DIGESTING LIFE
CREATING AWARENESS

First Published by Brolga Publishing Pty Ltd 2012
PO Box 12544 A'Beckett St Melbourne Australia 8006
ABN 46 063 962 443
email: sales@brolgapublishing.com.au
web: www.brolgapublishing.com.au

National Library of Australia Cataloguing-in-Publication entry

    Johanna Engwerda
    Digesting Life, Creating Awareness
    ISBN 9781922036469 (pbk.)

Printed in China
Cover design by David Khan
Typesetting by Angela Shi

BE PUBLISHED

Publish Through a Successful Australian Publisher
National Distribution
Enquiries to Brolga Publishing
Email: bepublished@brolgapublishing.com.au

Digesting Life
Creating Awareness

JOHANNA ENGWERDA

For all those fellow journeyers and seekers, may this book assist and inspire further momentum and growth.

*And for Anna, Katherine, Michael and Damian,
and for my loving husband Piet,
in gratitude and love.*

ACKNOWLEDGEMENTS

I wish to thank all those who have taught me meditation, either through direct teaching, intuitive experiences or through written texts. Many of these teachers are people I will never meet and many have passed over.

Thanks go to my first Tibetan Vajrayana teacher Catherine Jetsun Yeshe (Rathbun) for introducing me to Tibetan Buddhist meditation. I also thank Eric Harrison for encouragement and inspiration and Ian Gawler for lessons in simplicity of practice.

To my Dharma sisters both in Western Australia and in Canada who have travelled sections of the path with me – I value your friendship and shared values and support.

To Angela Durey, my spiritual and philosophical sounding board and very dear friend – I honour you.

To my Jungian dream analyst: Rhys Brown – my gratitude for showing me new ways to develop.

To my complementary spiritual friend and qigong teacher: Lyndal Galloway – thank you for sharing your knowledge, love and experience so freely.

To my students whom I have taught meditation over the years – you have helped me to learn how to teach and many of my teaching meditations have arisen whilst teaching you.

To Dr David Tadj – for having the vision, encouragement and drive to work with me over the years, in bringing meditation into acceptance as a complement to Western medicine.

To my dear husband Piet – thanks for your love and support always and for accepting my deep interest in meditation and dream analysis.

And lastly but very importantly, to my children Anna, Katherine, Michael and Damian – thanks for being your wonderful and individual selves and for accommodating my spiritual interests into your younger lives without complaint and in fact, with encouragement.

CONTENTS

INTRODUCTION   3

CHAPTER 1: DIGESTING LIFE   7

CHAPTER 2: THE SEARCH FOR WHOLENESS   17

CHAPTER 3: AWARENESS OF BODY   31

CHAPTER 4: AWARENESS OF MIND   61

CHAPTER 5: AWARENESS OF DREAM AND THE SHADOW   87

CHAPTER 6: AWARENESS OF SUBTLE ENERGY   115

CHAPTER 7: AWARENESS IN RELATIONSHIP   151

CHAPTER 8: THE ESSENCE   181

APPENDIX A   199

APPENDIX B   203

APPENDIX C   207

BIBLIOGRAPHY   211

"The sole purpose of human existence is to kindle a light in the darkness of mere being."

Carl Jung. Memories. Dreams. Reflections.[1]

"The alchemical vessel is the context in which the forces released from the darkness can be held. However, transformation will seldom occur within this vessel without a particular quality of consciousness. When a tantric practitioner enters the vessel, a special awareness is needed to remain present, alert, and conscious to the energy generated as the life of the unconscious is activated. Without awareness there is unlikely to be transformation or integration. Instead we will find ourselves pulled into emotional habits and will be easily overwhelmed. One of the central obstacles to the effectiveness of any developmental path arises from a lack of awareness."

Rob Preece. The Psychology of Buddhist Tantra.[2]

1 C Jung, Memories, Dreams, Reflections, Collins, Routledge & P Kegan, London, 1963.
2. R Preece, The Psychology of Buddhist Tantra, Snow Lion Publications, New York, 2006, p.101.

INTRODUCTION

One day around the time of my birthday, something strange happened. In previous years I had noticed that unusual meditative experiences sometimes occurred around this time. A spiritual teacher once told me that it relates to the planetary influences around the time of one's birth. On the morning of this particular birthday, I happened to be doing my Tibetan Buddhist meditation practice of Guru Yoga when an insight flashed into my mind - literally - like a bolt of lightning. The insight was that I was going to write a book. The book was to be a reflection on my life's spiritual journey to date and a refining of the essence of what I have learnt from this journey.

My immediate reaction to this insight was an emphatic and instinctual 'No. It's much too hard. I can't do it. What do I know? There are already so many similar books out there, who would read another one?' I found myself thinking many negative thoughts, the general trend being a lack of confidence in my own ability to write, and I went back to my meditation practice, thinking that I had banished the idea and pleased that I had treated it with logic and realism. No sooner had I settled back into my practice than I received another abrupt mental jolt and this time the title of the book came loud and clear. It came not as words but as a very clear thought, Digesting Life. Ideas and thoughts then came streaming into my mind about the subjects, chapters and general theme of the book. I began to make a few notes in my meditation journal, which I kept next to me, and within a short space of time, I had the outline for this book.

This time I thought, 'Well, that's a good idea. Maybe such a book is possible,' and for a day or two I entertained the idea in a general sort of way. Soon though, I once again decided it was an impossible undertaking. I deeply feared the possibility of failure, of giving up midway through the writing of it, and of experiencing rejection if the book wasn't accepted. Several weeks later, I went to see my Jungian dream analyst with an assortment of dreams that I'd had the previous fortnight. One of those dreams was a clear message that I was taking the easy way out on some spiritual matter; that I was going back into my comfort zone and not trusting and following my spiritual truth. It didn't take long to interpret that the dream was referring to this book and my fear of writing it.

When my dream analyst had listened to my fears, he suggested that I write the book for myself and so I felt confident enough to begin writing.

The book reflects on twenty years of spiritual searching after the breakdown of my marriage, unusual events which occurred during my work in a public hospital as a registered nurse, meditation experiences which always inspired me to continue practicing, my issues with illness and healing and my extensive curiosity in psychology. These experiences led me to acquire a counselling qualification, to my practice of Jungian dream analysis as a source of wisdom and healing, to training as an Indian head massage therapist, to an overwhelming passion for Tibetan

Buddhist meditation and philosophy - particularly Vajrayana or Tantric meditation – and eventually to meditation teaching. I am also a mother of four children and parenting has been a huge wake up call for me, influencing my growth as a person through showing me both my shadow side and my compassionate side. Living in the world as a working single mother and then later remarrying, has also informed my life experiences. In many ways my life has been a typical modern life for a Westerner, with some extraordinary experiences thrown in!

This book attempts to crystallise and clarify what I've learnt from all my searching in the hope that it may be of benefit to others by inspiring them on their spiritual or self-development path.

CHAPTER ONE
DIGESTING LIFE

I began meditating almost by accident. I was attending a yoga class almost twenty years ago to try to find some mental peace in a time of great upheaval. At the end of the class our yoga teacher guided us through a body relaxation exercise and then instructed us all to sit around in a circle on the floor gazing at a candle in silence. I found this so fascinating that I began doing this every day in our tiny study, at home while my husband and four young children continued with their noise outside the door. Something in me realised that this new activity was very important and I persisted, with a little note pinned to the door saying that I was not to be disturbed! When I look back at those times, I wonder what seed was already present in me that knew exactly what I was doing and where I was going.

This gazing at a candle and keeping my attention on it was my first mindfulness practice using an object. From there I began reading books on meditation and over the next several years, progressed to body relaxation, body scanning and breath practices. At one point I followed a Perth meditation teacher called Eric Harrison as I was much impressed by his little book *Do You Want To Meditate?*[3] As a consequence of doing these practices daily I found a degree of peace of mind, at least when I was meditating and sometimes at other times. Later, I did further work with Ian Gawler in Melbourne and attended various meditation workshops by other teachers, particularly Buddhist. Breath meditation practices now became my focus and gradually I began to experience deep levels of stillness. After six years of working with breath practices on my own and fairly exclusively, I began to realise intuitively that I had gone as far as I could without a teacher and I began searching for one. As fate would have it, I met one within the year – a visiting Canadian Lama by the name of Catherine Jetsun Yeshe (Rathbun). She had been trained in the Kagyu lineage of Tibetan Buddhism.[4] This lineage is particularly interested in the practice of meditation. This was my introduction to Tibetan Mahayana and Vajrayana practices. I studied and practiced with her both in Australia and Canada for five years, quite intensely.

For many years I have continued to use Tibetan Buddhist practices that use ritual text, visualisation and mantra. They continue to inspire me even after doing them daily for many years. They nourish me in a deeply spiritual way, re-energise me, re-motivate me to continue with my aspiration towards wholeness and love, and allow wisdom to filter through into my consciousness so that I am given clarity and assistance about my life on a daily basis. To be able to experience deep peace and stillness on a daily basis is something that I am continually grateful for. It is a welcome freedom from the compulsive habit of self-preoccupation.

Now, many years after beginning Tibetan practices I am returning to incorporating mindfulness practice into everything that I do. I realise that mindfulness/awareness practice is the basis of all practices. All the practices and theories we try during our search for wholeness give us a framework on which to hang

3 E Harrison, *Do You Want To Meditate?* Self published, Perth, Western Australia, 1991.
4 C Rathbun, *Clear Heart, Open Mind*, Friends of the Heart, Toronto, 2008.

future practices and theories. We can compare the effect of one with the other and build our knowledge of what is helpful and what is not. We experience many things before we learn the essence. When we start to feel the quality of groundedness or centeredness entering our lives, then we see the value of mindfulness practice. Ironically it is not until we begin to develop this quality that we can see the value of it.

After the idea of a book first came to me I soon had another dream which made me wake up to the fact that I was continuing to avoid a difficult task (I can be fiercely resistant to change!). Once I had acknowledged the message of the dream and made a firm commitment in the early hours of the morning to start writing this book that very day, I went back to sleep. I dreamt a dream of creating abundance and sustenance from very ordinary and easily obtained basic materials. How simple it really is to create, said the dream, once you know how to transform the ordinary into the extraordinary. We all live lives which are simultaneously ordinary and extraordinary – hidden beneath every ordinary process something extraordinary is happening. It is through personal transformation that we come to be aware of the presence of both and to set about integrating them.

Life, cunningly, presents us with opportunities to work on our issues and so, gradually to transform ourselves. If we look back at our life's pattern, we see how these events and opportunities repeat themselves over and over again. For instance, we may be in the habit of doing easy tasks first and leaving difficult tasks till last. This indicates a lack of confidence in our own abilities. Other people only do what they want to do, what they can control or what they can be a success at, and most people tend not to challenge themselves unless they absolutely have to. Life is difficult enough, we think. Why make life more difficult for ourselves?

Digestion is usually thought of as a process whereby we attempt to assimilate into our body food that we have already eaten. It is a passive process, not requiring our active attention. We digest our food that is then transformed into energy. It is possible to treat life as such a passive process, absorbing what happens without paying too much attention.

This conceptual attitude of being the passive receiver may be tied in with attitudes which have us believing that we can't change ourselves or what happens to us. But life doesn't have to be like this. We can eat or partake of life consciously, in an aware way, and so take part in life actively, rather than be tossed and turned by it as though life is a wild storm. Awareness is the key. Being aware of events happening as they happen in the moment and gradually absorbing their meaning, we enable self-transformation to occur.

The following quote from Lama Anagarika Govinda's mesmerising book, *The Way of the White Clouds*[5], never ceases to inspire me.

> "Just as a white summer cloud, in harmony with heaven and earth freely floats in the blue sky from horizon to horizon following the breath of the atmosphere - in the same way the pilgrim abandons himself to the breath of the greater life that...leads him beyond the farthest horizons to an aim which is already present within him, though yet hidden from his sight."

As Lama Govinda so poetically expresses, much of our understanding of ourselves and our lives is 'hidden from our sight' and it is not until we abandon our need to control life and learn to trust in the process that we begin to develop the quality of awareness and our lives can be brought up into the light of consciousness. The process of digesting life is the process of gaining awareness.

5 Lama Anagarika Govinda, *The Way of the White Clouds*, Rider, London. 1995.

We may be unclear about how to achieve personal change and transformation. Firstly, if we want to create lasting change we must be able to accept that this change will involve persistent effort as well as learning how to accept responsibility for our lives. It is all too easy to deny the existence of our repetitive faults or blame them on others and we need a certain degree of self-awareness to start the process of change within ourselves. Self-development is closely connected with self-healing, and spirituality is a well-known path for personal transformation. This process is a gradual one however. Some people dedicate years and years of time and practice to attempting to achieve this aim with often slow progress. What we notice is that if this intention for spiritual or personal transformation does not take first place in the queue of life's tasks, it becomes even less likely that there will be progress. Transformation requires patience, motivation, discipline and support but it has the capacity to be the most worthwhile thing we accomplish during our lifetime.

At the root of transformation is recognition of the desire to change. This is number one. Also helpful is a realistic attitude about the time it takes to bring about change. It takes time to change neurological pathways in the brain – to create new behavioural circuits. The heart takes time to soften. There is a physical as well as an emotional, spiritual and psychological component to change. We shouldn't be put off by slow progress or no apparent progress, because if we have the intention to change then change is already happening through the force of our motivation. Even thoughts of changing create energy pathways in the brain which affect other energy pathways. In my experience a daily spiritual practice, no matter how small, is very conducive to bringing about gradual change. As well as increasing one's self-awareness, it gives one an anchor, something still and centred to come back to, time and time again, amidst the joys and trials of life.

Being on this earth can be a curse, a great joy and many places in between. Life is always unpredictable. But the one great thing about being on this earth is that in this lifetime we have unlimited opportunities to grow as a person, to learn, to develop, to improve and to use our gifts for our own happiness and for the benefit of others. Even a small positive change in our mental outlook immediately affects many people whom we may live with, work with, or spend time with, and that is before we consider our own increased life satisfaction and happiness. So this book is not about making big changes. This book is about changing the little things slowly and with persistence. That's all we're meant to do. No big feats. No big accomplishments. Small barely perceptible changes – that's how it works.

When I first started on my spiritual search many years ago, I had two visions which illustrate this process of change in our lives. I have remembered these visions often over the years when sometimes I have bemoaned the slow progress happening with regard to personal change.

Molecules Passing Through a Wall

The first vision (or dream), which occurred in the state between waking and sleeping – the hypnogogic state – was a strange mental image of molecules passing through a thick wall. I could see inside the wall from the side view and I was watching the molecules passing through, one by one, from one side to the other. A thought immediately came into my mind of how incredibly and painstakingly slow the process of moving millions of molecules from one side of the wall through to the other was. How many thousands of years it would take for the molecules to move to the other side! I was absolutely astounded and impressed by the vision. I realised that I had been shown the truth; it felt incredibly real.

To explain this vision – change happens molecule by molecule. For each piece of knowledge gained, we must put that piece into motion. Change takes time and repetition. We must be patient and understand that each small step is small progress but progress none the less. Without the movement of each miniscule molecule, the end result of all the millions of particles reaching the other side of the wall will never occur. This process happens for every small change we may try to make. When we look at recent research into how the brain changes itself, we see how the neuronal circuits which have evolved with our conditioning, both in this life and during our evolution as a species, have come about. We also see that these neuronal circuits are not easily changed; in fact some of them never are, despite them being counterproductive.[6] However, in Norman Doidge's book, *The Brain that Changes Itself*, we read that scientific research is showing that change in our thinking, emotions and behaviour is definitely possible and this is very encouraging for us.[7]

Walls Crumbling

The second vision occurred in a dream. It was an image of a thick circular stone wall, like a fortress, standing all alone in a silent landscape. It reminded me of the Walls of Jericho in the Bible. At first there were a few small holes developing in the wall. As I watched, much time passed – hundreds of years, perhaps. From time to time, I noticed little chips of rock flying off the wall here and there. Over much time, holes appeared in different parts of the wall. All this happened very slowly. One day, after many long silent years and the creation of multiple holes and chips in the wall, there was a loud sound, a rumbling, and slowly the massive walls began to topple. As I watched, I realised that all the little holes had caused sufficient weaknesses in the structure of the wall to make it crumble all at the same time. From watching the process day by day there had been no indication that the wall would topple so suddenly. It was an impressive sight and a lesson which made a huge impression on me. Once again it felt like the truth and very real.

6 J LeDoux, *The Emotional Brain*, Phoenix. London, 1999, p. 203.
7 See N Doidge, *The Brain That Changes Itself,* Scribe Publications, Melbourne, 2008.

To help explain this vision – change is a continual process of wearing away old patterns. We may not see any change happening or we may think that the change is too minor to achieve anything. We can't see the whole wall of life from where we are. Nevertheless, there will come a day when all the little wearings away reach a threshold point, when enough change has occurred to bring about a huge shift. Of course there was change happening from the making of the first little hole, but we couldn't see the result of that until many little holes had been worn away and eventually the combined force of all this accumulated small change caused a big change – the wall to topple.

These two visions came to me many years ago and I am still working on change and personal transformation. I don't think that process will ever end in my lifetime. As we become more and more aware of ourselves, our lives and our relationships, we find more and more to adjust and improve. The goal is to begin and to maintain the process, not necessarily to reach the end, because there is no end.

When I first started examining my life, my marriage of eighteen years had just finished with great emotional turmoil. I understood then, quite suddenly, that I had been asleep all of my life up until that point. I had this insight that I hadn't been living in the real world at all. This major event was a huge wake-up call, forcing me to begin looking at myself and my effect on others. This was the beginning of my 'awareness' training. It is said that we teach what we most need to learn; for me, my life's journey has been about slowly cultivating awareness. As have many other people, I have been given huge pointers to force me to change and learn. Now I have a much more stable way of life and I have the time to look at what I have experienced and learnt. In a way, my life up until now has been a gradual process of digestion and a struggle to begin the process of waking up and of recreating myself. It is a process that continues every day of my life.

All human beings on this earth have faults and are imperfect. We all have positive, negative and neutral aspects to our natures; and the fact that we have faults doesn't make us bad people. Having faults, once they are acknowledged, is the beginning of either change or acceptance. Owning up to our own faults also helps us to understand others who have faults. Most importantly, having faults keeps us humble and we realise that we are no better than anyone else – we are all in this together. However, it is worthwhile remembering what the Chinese philosopher Lao Tzu said, that if we don't change direction, we will end up where we are going. These are wise words.

I believe it is true that we create our lives each day. Our thoughts, attitudes, actions and motivations have a great influence on the upcoming events of our lives. It is not difficult to see this in our lives and the lives of others. We are quite capable of changing direction; we are the creators of our lives, often without even realising it. We have immense potential and are more powerful than we know. Transformation, however, requires a container or a context in which it can happen and there are many paths that we can follow depending on our individual needs. Many of our qualities are undeveloped or unconscious and require a structure of some sort to help them emerge. It is our responsibility in this life to explore both our outer and inner worlds equally and then finally to merge them, so that we can heal and transform ourselves according to our own truth.

CHAPTER TWO
THE SEARCH FOR WHOLENESS

For many people there is at times an intuitive feeling that we are not complete; and with regards to our lives, it is not uncommon to feel that there is something missing. From time to time this emptiness can result in periods of depression, worthlessness and hopelessness. This feeling of lack may drive us towards a search for greater self-knowledge and meaning in our lives or it may drive us towards the use of other means to fill the emptiness including: sex, busyness, relationships, alcohol, food, drugs, stimulants or other addictions. We find however, after a time, that these things do not necessarily solve the problem; they do not provide a lasting feeling of completion or self-worth. Learning how to fill our ill-defined missing areas is not easy and requires us to do some serious reflecting.

Some spiritual disciplines teach that we are already whole and perfect just as we are, but these words tend not to ring true if we can't relate to them. It may be that we have been taught by implication during our lives that we are not perfect, not good and in fact we have probably learnt, rightly or wrongly, that we are severely lacking in many personal areas. For some people this outer criticism has turned inwards so that there is an inner critic, a little voice that judges negatively all that we do. Depression feeds on this inner critic. Many deep emotions and learned patterns of behaviour need to be brought into our awareness before we can come to the truth of who we really are.

As we process all these deep undercurrents, we may go through a challenging time of not really liking who we are. In truth, it is rare to meet someone who is perfectly comfortable with who they are. This feeling of completion or wholeness is therefore simply a theory for most people. The practicality of being content and complete, is probably only experienced when we are reunited with loved ones after an absence, when we come to our physical home (or bed) to rest, or when we are in a state of deep meditation or other mystical experience.

This does not deter us from seeking the experience however. Intimate relationships are commonly used in this quest to feel whole. Most of us also look for objects, people and events which we believe will make us happy. Throughout history drug and alcohol-taking have been used for this purpose: to relax, to calm, to escape life, to make us feel strong, powerful and fulfilled. Ingesting these chemicals into our bodies alters our body chemistry and our perception of self. We feel changed, sometimes for the better. However, it is an artificial and temporary self-transformation and is not long lasting and there are also numerous, undesirable side effects. If we want the experience of wholeness to be ours in a healthy long lasting way, it is necessary to first learn about ourselves and why we act, think and feel the way that we do. This is sometimes called 'inner work'.

Inner work takes many forms all of which involve learning about self and our place in the world, e.g. philosophy, psychology, spirituality, dream work and meditation to name a few. It is quite possible to use relationships and work environments in the context of inner work if we aim to observe how we relate to others and then reflect deeply on what we find. The most important areas which usually need attention are our minds and our hearts and we may try many spiritual disciplines or therapists until we find something that suits our personality and our belief system. It is also possible to learn much from reading some of the excellent psychological and spiritual books which are so widely available. Psychology essentially means a study of the normal mind and spirituality essentially means a study of the mind, heart, ethics and philosophy combined. Some disciplines teach that there is nothing that needs changing, whereas other disciplines teach a quite structured path which shows how to go about finding inner peace or completion.

My first experiences of completion came with moments of awe outside in nature. All of a sudden the light became magical, the colours extra clear, the sounds intense, the view exquisite. It was a feeling of time stopping still, of wonder, of bliss and of needing nothing. Everything felt complete and perfect. Many people can relate to this essentially spiritual experience. I have heard my son, a surfer, explain his experience with being in the ocean in a way that shows this same feeling of 'oneness', awe or completion. A similar feeling can be experienced in meditation. What is actually happening is that we are experiencing moments of deep contentment without the ego being present. We are not thinking or analysing, we are simply experiencing. This then is completion, a sense of coming home to our true nature or what Buddhists call 'natural mind' – the essence of who we really are.

Change is both ongoing and constant in our lives, present in our external environment, our home life, our work life, our emotions, our opinions, our intellect and understanding, our wisdom, our awareness, our families, our friends, our bodies and our minds. Change occurs on so many levels. Buddhist philosophy states that everything in our universe is constantly changing and is therefore inherently impermanent. The word they use for this concept is 'impermanence'. If we look at ourselves we see that our body cells keep replacing themselves and changing – hair cells, skin, height and weight. In addition our diet, stress levels, health issues, feelings about things, likes and dislikes are all capable of change, some from moment to moment. Even trying to find out what sort of a person we really are is an impossible task. There is no one unchanging person and who we present to the world or how we see ourselves is often just our ego layer. We are constantly changing and adapting to the environment and the people around us. Buddhists have a name for this also – 'emptiness'. This means that no one and nothing exists as a solid, unchanging and permanent entity and things only exist in relationship to other things.

Tibetan Buddhist teachings, however, state that we have an unchanging 'Buddha nature' in each of us. Buddha nature is the part of us that has the possibility or potentiality for enlightenment or complete awareness. Enlightenment is the Buddhist equivalent of completion or wholeness. It seems that this seed of possibility is an unchanging part of us, and in this particular tradition it is described as a form of internal energy or consciousness that continues on after our physical form dies.

Other traditions have also attempted to make sense of the unchanging part of the individual human being, for example in the Christian tradition it is called a soul, and in Hinduism it is called a monad. Many explanations exist. There remains much confusion about terminology and there is no one clear explanation.

What Buddhists advocate is that if one wishes to work on loosening the shackles of habit, ignorance and past conditioning and one works on transforming oneself, it is possible to live more in tune with one's true nature.

What Commonly Propels us on our Search?

Some people embark on the path of spiritual learning after experiencing a life-changing, spontaneous spiritual experience such as an out of body experience, a near death experience, an experience of mystical oneness, feelings of intense and unexplained bliss, a moment of illumination or deep insight, or many other forms of spontaneous unusual happening. Some people embark on the search out of a deep curiosity to know more about life and death, perhaps triggered by an outer event. Many of us, however, embark on a reappraisal of life when we are faced with major suffering or the inexplicable in life and we are looking for a change in our circumstances. Unwanted health issues, a broken heart after a relationship ends, or mental suffering of many kinds – these and similar events are a call to awareness, to wake up to our lives and to stop living our life as if it were a dream.

From the Buddhist perspective, our ability to experience both pain and pleasure leads us to search for knowledge and more understanding about our existence here on earth. The search also comes about because of our deep desire to overcome suffering and find happiness.[8]

We are, in fact, very fortunate when things go majorly wrong because misfortune can motivate us to re-evaluate our mortality and our usefulness and our reason for being on this planet. Misfortune, if we don't permanently succumb to deadening our pain with inappropriate measures, can propel us to begin looking for the meaning in our individual and collective lives.

Mental and emotional suffering initially may predispose us towards wasting much time with our minds continually living in the past or the future rather than the present. Our thoughts are on who or what has caused our pain or on how we can avoid

8 Kalu Rinpoche, *The Dharma*, State University of New York Press, 1986, pp.13-42.

pain in the future. Pain and suffering has the ability to make us very introverted and self-protective. It is said that pain causes us to regress and we may find ourselves acting as we did when we were children. This applies to many types of pain. For instance, if the pain we feel is emotional, we will typically respond to the situation in the same way that we learnt to respond to similar pain as a child. Once we begin to observe our patterns of behaviour however, we may learn that there are different ways to respond to pain and misfortune.

Failed relationships can have a very powerful effect on us. They have the ability to devastate us, at least for a time. We can become very dependent on relationships with others to make us feel that we exist and that we have value. Subconsciously we feel that if someone else acknowledges our presence then we must exist. On the other hand, relationships provide meaning, intimacy, comfort and human connection. A problem typically arises if the relationship is used to fill some inner void. We expect the other person to make us feel whole and happy. Of course this only appears to happen in the initial stages of a romantic relationship and soon we find that the inner void still exists. If this relationship should fail, one party at least will suffer a significant loss and their view of reality and themself can be altered drastically. This is often the time for immense self-reflection.

Another life challenge which may propel us towards philosophical questioning can be when people retire from the workforce. It is then quite apparent that the world continues on its way quite happily without us. We may even experience a sense of complete insignificance which can be challenging indeed. These deep existential questions are not easily answered and each of us must come to our own understanding of who we are and what it is that we want to learn and do with our lives. It appears that humans will continue to search for some reason for life, above and beyond day-to-day existence because our human consciousness has evolved to the point where we can evaluate our lives. This is the price we pay for having complex and evolved brains. We are acutely aware of the limit and duration of our lives on this planet.

How Long Does the Search Take?

Once begun, most people say that this search goes on like an unstoppable train and there is no getting off. In fact, the search gathers momentum and we feel we will never finish. The search expands into ever widening circles until we may get lost in the complexity of it. We begin to question it all. Have we learnt anything or are we back where we started from so many years ago? This point of getting to a stage of complete unknowing marks significant opening and this can happen again and again. Ultimately and repeatedly we will return to this state of unknowing and each time we develop more humility and become more grounded and realistic about what we have learnt along the way. We learn more and more to let go of expectations and results and we learn to see without delusion and through the veils of ignorance. Each day lived with increasing awareness means progress. It is each day that is important, not the idea of a goal when we supposedly reach perfection.

Potential Dangers of the Search

A familiar problem for those who begin spiritual searching or who become involved in inner work is that we develop a desperation to try everything, hoping that one of these will be the magic cure to heal all our past hurts and make us happy. We may spend thousands of dollars on our search. We may read hundreds of books. We may listen to many teachers from many traditions. We can go on searching in an addictive type of way and not know how to stop, or recognise, what is useful and what is not. This desire for more and more is similar to how we live our lives. We unconsciously think that if one thing makes us happy then ten of those things will make us even happier. We rush to the next workshop or teacher. The Buddhists call this tendency 'desire' or 'attachment' – wanting this and wanting that.[9] Buddhist masters say that pleasure and excitement is not lasting and that soon it is gone and then we are left with ourselves again. Ironically, when we begin our search we use the same strategies that got us into trouble in the first place. The search becomes yet another way of shifting responsibility so that we don't have to confront the facts.

This search for wholeness can be extremely time-consuming and we may not be aware that we are involved in the search as an escape from life. If we are not careful, our searching can take us away from spending time with family members, friends, our children and our social lives. It can lead us to idolise teachers to both their and our detriment. It can make us dependent on others who may or may not have more spiritual knowledge than we have. The spiritual search has its pitfalls and we must be aware of them. Ultimately it is an 'alone' search from the point of view that no one else is able to do it for us – no teacher, no partner, no mystical guide and no good friend, but that does not mean that we should withdraw from family and friends. No one will achieve full awareness without the help of, or the interaction with others. It is also respectful to acknowledge that everyone goes along different pathways. What is relevant for one person is irrelevant for another; we each have our own lessons to learn.

Spirituality, with its feelings of love and compassion, can make us feel better in difficult times. There is no problem in using spirituality to balance our thoughts and emotions but a difficulty arises when we neglect real life problems because we feel powerless to change them or we neglect everyday life because we think it is trivial and unimportant.

In times past, spiritual teachers would cloister themselves away for huge periods of time to reflect and meditate. Their

9 Dilgo Khyentse, *The Heart Treasure of The Enlightened Ones*, Shambhala, Boston, 1992, p 129.

culture supported them to do that. It is uncommon for us in the modern world however, to choose this path and a huge part of our spiritual path will involve learning how to interact with others. Real everyday life is important. It is our testing ground and the environment in which we exist and no amount of spirituality will help us if we refuse to relate to others and to our world. With global communication now being almost instant, this is one of the main challenges of our era and it is imperative for the survival of our species and our earth that we learn these lessons of living harmoniously together.

Discouragement during the search will happen and when this presents itself we simply observe the process. We stay with it and we wait until our thoughts change again. When we become discouraged it often means that we become discouraged with our own ability to face life. There may be periods when we deeply question our usefulness in this life. When we lose motivation to keep going, as we will, we can recognise it as a pattern that we may have repeated over and over. We can recognise that it will pass when the emotions pass and that the emotions are just created complexes. Despite the fact that we lose motivation, wisdom about the next step will come – we simply need to be patient. This is the time to keep setting aside a period every day for quiet time – reading, reflection, movement meditation or just sitting in silence.

Regular Reassessment

It is important every now and again to stop and reassess where we are going with our search for self and spiritual development and to see where we have been. I have found it helpful, at regular intervals, to spend a few hours quietly reading over my entries in a meditation journal that I keep next to me during meditation. This is not a personal journal; this is a record of my spiritual learning, thoughts, insights and experiences. In it I also record any life difficulties and how they relate to my spiritual journey.

I periodically note the main themes. I note what I have learnt and what I am still working on and I note the wonderful things that occur during the quest for self-knowledge. Reading over the journal makes me rejoice in my journey and it supports my progress. Out of this regular stocktake, I see more clearly which direction to take my spiritual and worldly practice in. This comparison of the spiritual and the relational is a good habit to get into. It is easy to keep travelling in the same direction despite it no longer being effective, simply because we have not made the time to look back or because we are trying to please someone else, rather than connecting with our own inner wisdom.

Continual reassessment is necessary simply because life is continually changing and us with it. The people we were two years ago are probably different in many respects from the people we are today even though this is difficult to see at times. Change is the surest sign of growth, however if we focus on the results of practice, our attention is taken away from the moment to moment experience and learning. After many years of searching we realise that salvation or cure is not out there as we had initially hoped, but we do gradually gain in strength, courage, resilience, compassion, tolerance, wisdom and love – these are the types of qualities that we are searching to develop.

And then of course, when we do develop these qualities momentarily, they will frustratingly disappear when we most need them. We so easily slip back into the way we have always been. I still have a long way to go. Sometimes I reflect on how many thousands of hours I have spent on reading, contemplation and spiritual practices and wonder how many university degrees I could have achieved by this time if I had spent an equivalent amount of time and energy on university study instead. But then at particular moments when I am filled with grace (a sense of being blessed), I realise the value and significance of spiritual and inner work. I truly feel that this is the most worthwhile thing I've ever learnt in my life. I, and others who walk the spiritual path, know that this is the work that we will take with us beyond the grave and that nothing else will survive. One of the most wonderful things about embarking on the search is that one becomes infused with a wish to make things better for others as well as ourselves. We feel change happening in the heart and we more acutely feel our interconnectedness with others. It is the realignment of the heart and the mind together that seems to produce remarkable changes.

How Do We Focus on What's Important and Not Get Diverted?

Recently my mind presented me with yet another intriguing image during meditation. In this vision I saw moisture from the atmosphere changing form. It swirled, transformed into liquid and dripped down into the wide mouth of a funnel which was positioned over an open square container. I watched the liquefied moisture make its way through the narrower part of the funnel and settle into the bottom of the container. I saw clearly that any large matter mixed with the liquid would be blocked from entering the container by the narrow mouth of the funnel. I saw also that the container could only hold a finite amount of liquid – beyond this the liquid overflowed. Additionally, I saw that the liquid, through being contained, was now changed. It now had a context to give it meaning and structure.

The vision once again had that 'real' quality to it, meaning that it had a message for me.

I speculated. The blocking of large particles of matter from flowing through the funnel also reminded me of the process of digestion. Larger particles cannot flow through unless they are broken down into smaller particles first. Could this image be telling me that information needs to be absorbed in manageable-sized portions? Could it also mean that it's the little things that are important as they alone gain entry? The container is of limited capacity, it can only hold so much – at some point we have to stop pouring things in because we can only assimilate and integrate a finite amount. After that limit is reached, information is wasted. Do we really need to ingest everything? Are we going to have room for it all? Will the excess of information make us sick?

The funnel image has immediate parallels to the search and, in fact, to any type of learning. At some point we simply have to stop trying to push many self-development practices into a finite container. It doesn't achieve anything to have the container overflowing. We are simply not digesting or able to use anything that overflows. We need to be able to condense the important learning into a container with manageable boundaries and with some sort of meaning to it. Therefore, to choose a spiritual tradition or practice to follow must be our first decision. This provides a context for transformation.

Our life span is also limited. Time will run out and at some point we must try to make sense of all we have learnt and to find for ourselves what is really important. Contrary to our society's way of more and more, on the spiritual path we need to one day come to the place of crystallisation. We need to try to make things simple and clear. It benefits us to make sure that we are focused on what we find is useful to us at a particular time. A simple practice, short or long, which we understand and we are able to use every day is all we need. One practice, no matter how simple, done regularly is much more effective than scattering our energy far and wide without much effort or understanding.

As we continue with inner work and begin to see the need for change incorporating more than just the spiritual, contemplative, psychological or meditative approach, we may find ourselves adding to our daily spiritual practice. We will begin to do 'outer work' – improve our external environment and perhaps our living conditions, type of work, relationships or general health. Even if we are involved in many of these areas at once, both inner and outer, we need to be mindful of keeping things simple and not having the sense of rushing through them. Better to take things slowly and learn well.

CHAPTER THREE
AWARENESS OF BODY

In ancient cultures, indigenous people revered the body and its sexuality and their connection with nature and the earth. Strict and puritanical religions from the sixteenth century instilled in populations the idea that the body was impure and its workings uncouth. Later, sexuality became a hidden and furtive subject. Many of these attitudes have remained up until the present time, even in our younger and apparently more sexually liberated generations. Understanding how the body and sexuality function have been almost exclusively the domain of medical personnel, although in the last decade more research about the body is being published.

In light of the above, it is understandable that many of us have little insight into how important our body is and we have even less awareness of our body from moment to moment. It is as though our thoughts and emotions control our lives and the body is expected to simply follow. We have a body-mind split which is very successfully instilled in our Western group consciousness. People who embark on the self-development path soon notice that much emphasis is placed on learning awareness of thoughts and emotions rather than on our bodies, and this bias is especially prominent in psychological therapy. In our outer lives, we have little training in learning body awareness unless we aim to excel in a particular sport and even then, the body's needs will most likely be subjugated to the will (or mind) of the sportsman/woman.

Traditional meditation such as in the Hinayana Buddhist tradition, has attempted to teach mindfulness of the body through practices which encourage us to see the body and physical matter as the foundation of suffering, i.e. practitioners were taught to deny or transcend the body in the interests of being 'spiritual'. Originally many practices evolved in which practitioners were instructed to visualise their decaying or impermanent bodies.[10]Repulsion for the body through such meditations were intended to suppress sexuality in monks, many of them young, so that their minds would not stray from spiritual practice.

In the Buddhist Tantric tradition however, the view of the body was quite different.[11] Here the body and its elemental energies were considered sacred and to be used as vehicles for transformation. Sexuality and even eroticism were included in this type of meditation because of the powerful inner energies associated with sexuality. Many of these practices were considered secret and were hidden from most practitioners. Sexual energy however is not the only type of inner energy associated with the body's processes. The Chinese Traditional Medicine view of the body incorporated many documented pathways along which this subtle energy or 'chi' travelled. Buddhist Tantra, which understands that the body and mind are linked by subtle energy,

10 V Wallace, & A Wallace, *A Guide to The Bodhisattva's Way of Life by Santideva*, Snow Lion, New York, 1997, pp. 93-98.
11 Preece, pp. 75-86.

has been mistakenly viewed as focusing only on sexuality, when in fact it focuses on all types of subtle or inner energy. Tantra or Vajrayana does not deny awareness of the body and in fact practices involve linking the body feelings with subtle energy.

When people in Western countries begin learning meditation, they are often initially taught body relaxation techniques such as progressive muscle relaxation or body scanning.[12] These Western body relaxation techniques are usually taught as a precursor for learning how to quieten the mind and sometimes they are taught as a method to promote healing in the body.[13] In my experience, these practices appear to work well for the purposes mentioned, at least during the meditation session, but somehow we continue to dissociate our bodies from our minds as we go about the busyness of our day. Learning about body awareness is perhaps one of the most difficult lessons we may have to learn during our lives. We have an entire societal culture around denying the existence and the 'aliveness' of the body.

This is not to say that we shouldn't use the body in meditation. The body makes a very useful focus for meditating and can gradually help us to be more aware of the sensations of the body as they arise.[14] The body exists very much in the present moment, therefore it is a good and simple focus for mindfulness meditation. For example: just sensing the feelings in the fingers of one hand by concentrating our full attention on them and how they feel for several minutes to the exclusion of all else, helps us to bring our mind into the present moment. We could say that we are learning to pay deliberate attention. This is mindfulness of the body.

As an example, see *Appendix A* for a simple meditation that uses the sensations of the body as a focus.

---

12 E Harrison, *Do You Want To Meditate?* Perth Meditation Centre, Western Australia, 2002.
13 I Gawler, *Meditation: Pure and Simple*, Hill of Content, Melbourne, 1996.
14 Namgyal Rinpoche, *The Breath of Awakening*, Bodhi Publishing, Ontario, 1992.

Body based movement meditations – such as yoga, tai chi, martial arts and qigong – are other techniques traditionally taught to people following a spiritual path. Such movement meditation has the additional benefit of helping people to experience the body's inner energies.[15] Movement meditations, when carried out with attention to the sensations in the different parts of the body, can help to develop mindfulness of the body, its balance and internal energy, and can elicit feelings of great peace. These types of meditations, rather than sitting meditations, may be more effective for some people because it is relatively easy to notice when one's mind has become distracted from the movements of the body. In meditation we aim to keep the mind focused on one thing in order to calm it – the body appears to be such a simple focus for our attention.

Awareness of energy patterns in and around the body is really awareness of the body on a much subtler level and here we begin to see the connection between the body and the mind. This aspect of body is not physical but is energetic or psychic in nature and it involves paying attention to inner sensations related to the psychic centres or 'chakras' and the channels and the pathways of the subtle energy system. Most authors continue to use Eastern terminology when describing subtle energy because western scientists haven't yet discovered a satisfactory scientific explanation of subtle energy in the body, although some attempt to explain it in terms of the sympathetic and autonomic nervous systems.[16] In Eastern traditions, it is known that our body is intimately related to this system of energy and that this system in turn is intimately related to the mind so that we have a very close body/mind connection. We will discuss subtle energy in a subsequent chapter.

---

15 Lam Kam Chuen, *The Way of Energy*, Gaia Books Ltd, New York, 1991.
16 E D'Aquili & AB Newberg, *The Mystical Mind, Probing the Biology of Mystical Experience*, Fortress Press, Minneapolis, 1999, p.25.

In my case, and in the case of countless other people, body awareness has begun to develop quite late in my life and mostly it has been forced on me by illness and injury. We seriously forget that the body is attached to our mind because mostly it seems to manage quite well without our awareness, up to a certain point – that is, until something goes wrong with it.

In my many years of meditation practice I was not successful in learning awareness of my body during my daily life. Definitely during meditation it was not difficult to be aware of the body and the breath, and mostly this was very relaxed and pleasurable, however this awareness never lasted much beyond the meditation cushion. It was not until my body began to fail me that I really began to learn about body awareness and how important it is to keep our awareness grounded in the body. Sooner or later we develop illnesses or injuries, major or minor, physical or psychological, which force us to stop what we are doing and adapt to changed circumstances. My greatest teacher about body awareness has been physical illness and injury.

For this reason I will not further discuss body based mediations, although they definitely have their place as a step towards developing mental stillness, rather I will write from my own experience as to what has finally bought body awareness to me.

Exploring Routine Health Problems

The aim of telling these stories is not to emphasise how to follow a process of medical diagnosis but rather to show how body awareness (and respect for it) arises eventually if we just take the time to listen or pay attention to our body. At all times, significant illness needs to be properly diagnosed by a medical doctor. If there is something wrong with the body it doesn't necessarily mean, however, that one needs an artificial chemical in the form of a prescription to fix it. This may be necessary in some cases but often the remedy is much simpler than that. We are all capable of looking within and being aware of how we are treating our body so that simple solutions may first be tried. For example, we hear often of people with influenza continuing to go to work when their body desperately need rest. Our body really is an amazing piece of technology, developed over millions of years, with the added bonus of having feelings, consciousness and intellect. The engine runs for approximately 82 years, it manufactures its own oil, it fights off invaders, it continually renews its protective cover, it is able to take in fuel from both food and the environment, it moves in a multitude of ways and is capable of reproducing itself. Can you imagine having to purchase a vehicle that could do all the things our body can do? We would be unable to afford such a vehicle.

As happens with most of us, we have a slight body problem that we ignore until at some point the illness or discomfort begins to affect our ability to complete our usual tasks: affecting our leisure activities or affecting the quality of our lives, and then we simply have to take notice. By the time the body makes us aware that something is wrong there is usually something hugely wrong.

Our mind also compensates and covers up what is happening with our body. We deny and procrastinate. Changing lifestyle and habits, after we become aware of what needs to change, is too hard. We tell ourselves that we don't have time or we will think about it later. However, eventually when something is seriously wrong we begin to take a serious interest. This can lead to investigating the illness by pursuing avenues of healing and various treatments. Some of us leave the treatment and decisions up to others, however some of us want to be in the driver's seat. Being in apparent control or letting others do the work for us, does not necessarily mean that we want to change. Both can be avenues of denying self-responsibility. It is not a comfortable experience to see and feel our body degenerating while we don't have the expertise or the knowledge to stop the process.

Or don't we? Let's see what happened in my case.

Health Problem One

I have had a particular ailment all my adult life: abdominal pain and discomfort. This spiralled out of control several years ago and required lots of attention.

I began experiencing stomach cramps that were so severe that I was forced to lie down. Then it would take one to two hours for the pain to stop. I had no idea what was causing the pain although I sensed that there was no point in going to the doctor and being a registered nurse helped me to look at my symptoms objectively. I had had a fairly clear colonoscopy only recently. My symptoms came irregularly and went away when I lay flat and I had no symptoms from other body systems; only the pain, abdominal bloating and at times the passage of excessive flatus. I was not losing weight or otherwise unwell. At the time, I didn't realise that I was mistreating my body. Hadn't my stomach always been difficult? It was a family thing. On and off, I experienced the symptoms. I told myself that I had to get used to all the horrible noises and smells emitting from my lower body – how embarrassing and humiliating all this was!

My life had begun to revolve around my stomach and the toilet and around hiding the symptoms from my co-workers. I couldn't wear anything snug or tight around my waist; definitely no belts. Still, I carried on and didn't change anything and I simply hoped the problem would go away and I wouldn't have to deal with it. I employed denial and avoidance, pure and simple. Please someone rescue me without me having to do a thing. Please let me keep doing the things that I want to do without giving anything up. Some of you may recognise this pattern in yourselves.

Eventually, I made a decision to take time off from my stressful job in order to try getting my body into balance. I made it my new job to investigate what was wrong with me. I really did want to feel well.

I visited a homeopath, a naturopath, a physiotherapist and a Bowen practitioner. I also spent more time on meditation. I made sure I slept enough, spent time out of doors, exercised daily and ate well. From the health professionals I got many and varied answers, probably all correct but the treatments and advice seemed to me to be only part of the answer. I was offered many pills and potions, supposedly natural. None of them made an appreciable difference. All these bits and pieces of causes and treatments weren't addressing the problem from a holistic point of view. I needed to find the whole story, not just angles of the story. I knew something important was missing from the picture.

One day I decided that after fifty-six years of living in my body I knew it better than anyone else, professional or not. My visit to the homeopath resulted in me keeping a food diary. I kept it religiously for several weeks. I started to observe my body as if it were a work project. I developed an exquisitely tuned 'ear' for any grumbles or changes. I learned how to pay attention and be fully aware. I kept a pain diary and documented exactly when, how bad, where, what relieved it, etc. This required me to notice and then record the findings. The results came quickly enough after that. I found that I couldn't eat fresh fruit with other food and then I found that I felt much better if I ate no fresh fruit at all. For someone who has been a fruitaholic this news was not what I wanted to hear. Still I was waking up to the fact that something drastic had to change and I had to be responsible for my own health.

I also found that when I cut out wheat products my stomach felt better still. My symptoms were really fading out of existence now. My stools were so normal that I couldn't recognise them as mine. I marvelled at them! Cutting out wheat for someone who has used bread and cheese as a staple diet was confronting to say the least, but now I was on the war path. I was going to cure myself. I was determined.

I found that it was important to listen to health professionals and obtain as much information as I could but ultimately I had to get to know my own body and know what suited it and what didn't. There is no point in eating two fruits and three vegetables every day if it causes pain.[17] I now know what I can and can't tolerate. How could anyone but me work all this out? How can we expect strangers to tell us what our body needs? Everybody is remarkably different and in the end we must understand that even our own brain can't be boss. We may really want to eat that piece of chocolate cake, our brain may desire it, but we must bow to the body that we have been given. We must respect it, honour it, treat it like a king or a queen.

It is helpful to remember that no matter how brilliant our mind, how spiritual our experiences, how successful we are seen to be – none of this is of any use if we don't have a body that enables us to function. Our body gives us the ability to stay alive and our brain gives us a basic consciousness. The body gives us the opportunity to use our talents and gifts and is the shell which encases our spirit. The traditional Tibetans knew this also. They went that bit further and said that digestion is the basis of good health. In my case this was true as digestion affected everything else in my life. So why hadn't I ever really listened to my body and developed awareness of it? Because I took my body for granted as so many people do and because I lived in my head, disconnected from my body.

As a nurse I had preached to patients about what a miracle the body is and I had mentioned to people that if we could only look inside we would be much more appreciative of its complexity and

17 Heart Foundation of Australia, Food and Nutrition Facts, retrieved 16 October 2011, <http://www. heartfoundation.org.au/healthy-eating/food-and-nutrition-facts/Pages/fruits-and-vegetables.aspx>

wonder. And I had always, since I was very young, had an interest in health: healthy food, exercise, not smoking, maintaining a healthy weight and being in the fresh air. I assumed that my body was healthy. Wasn't I some sort of health professional who knew what to do? It seems not. It took me many years to realise that I really wasn't giving my body the respect it was due. I wasn't listening to it and I had no awareness of it.

Another reason it took me so long to learn this lesson of awareness of the body is because doing so involved self-responsibility and change. I put up with the pain so that I could eat what I wanted. I loved the very things my body couldn't have. What a lesson in attachment to food and the gratification of desire. Finally, at some level my body was saying 'Enough! I have had more than my life's share of those foods. I can't cope with them any more'. My problem with my stomach and abdomen largely resolved itself very simply once I took on the responsibility of altering my diet. Of course there were other issues at play here. Most conditions require us to look at more than just diet but for now my big lesson here was awareness of my body and restraint.

Health Problem Two

Not long after I had worked through the abdominal issues I developed another condition – restless legs syndrome. I had once previously had this when I was pregnant. Now that I was more aware of my body I started to investigate more the nature and cause of this ailment as it was causing life-disrupting insomnia. All my working life I have been involved in the healing professions in one capacity or another, however this was the first time in my life that I had the opportunity to spend time putting all that I had learnt together. Even though we may not end up with all the answers or even cure ourselves, by working through the process of illness we come to a deeper understanding of its nature and our self.

The restless legs proved to be unpredictable and elusive. Its nature was very different from the stomach issues and it provided me with more to learn. Once again I tried the project approach. Focus on the issue, listen to the body, research current knowledge and treatments – surely I would succeed here too? Not so. As my Jungian dream analyst would say to me – we can't just use the 'Logos' approach (masculine) to work on our issues; we need to balance that with the 'Eros' approach (feminine). Whereas Logos is logical, scientific, active and definite; Eros is mysterious, elusive, intuitive and inconclusive. More recently we have come to understand this same concept in explaining the workings of the right and left hemispheres of the brain, both individually and together. Both hemispheres used together, provide a more complete or holistic way of looking at and dealing with life and ourselves.[18] This means that not only do we use our active brain to try to solve problems but that we also use our passive mind to reflect and wait so that wisdom, insight and intuition have the opportunity to arise from the other levels of our being.

Firstly, as regards the restless legs problem, I delved into the medical literature and then I visited a general medical practitioner. Neither was very encouraging. The condition's cause is unknown, its progress is usually progressive and there is no known cure. Usually it is managed with sedative and/or painkiller type medication.[19] When I tried such medication I found myself sedated during the day and I became constipated. The naturopathic path was to prescribe magnesium phosphate, which I tried without success. I then asked my qigong teacher for some exercises which might help me to work on possible energy blockages in the subtle energy system of the lower body but I discovered a mental resistance to doing these. I wanted help 'now' – I can be impatient.

18 I McGilchrist, *The Master and his Emissary: The Divided Brain and the making of the Western world,* Yale University Press, 2009
19 J Murtagh, *General Practice,* 3rd edit, McGraw-Hill, Australia, 2003, p.797.

I spoke with a retired medical doctor, who also suffered with restless legs and he passed on to me his theory that lymphatic massage of the legs and into the groin helps the condition as well as taking mild painkillers at night. He qualified what he said by saying that the massage had to be ongoing for many years and that there really wasn't a full cure of the condition and that different things worked for different people. Ah, I thought, perhaps the restless legs syndrome is due to the varicose veins in my right leg. That sounded plausible. One night, on a horror cheap red eye overnight flight across the country, jammed into a window seat and unable to move, I isolated the right leg as the culprit as it was the only leg affected by restlessness on the cramped plane. I began wearing a support stocking on the right leg overnight. This seemed to help.

A relative suggested a short term, tablet cure for the insomnia which was by now very distressing, as restless legs only affects people at night. What torture lack of sleep is! This I also tried but it played havoc with my sleep routine as I was left groggy in the morning and therefore this was not a long term solution. Some people suggested sedating homeopathic remedies at night. I tried everything. I found meditation had no effect on the condition. This is understandable as restless legs is a neurological condition. Walking at night worked brilliantly but one didn't get any sleep that way. Calf stretches before bed had some benefit.

Internet searches informed me that restless legs is a primary sleep disorder as well as a neurologically-based disorder. I was glad to hear that it was a sensorimotor disorder not a psychosomatic one – ego wouldn't have liked that! But why on earth had I got it now when I was well, relaxed and not working? I had mostly slept very well throughout my life, albeit a little more lightly as I got older. On the internet I learned restless legs might be caused by low iron levels in the blood but last time I had had my levels checked they were relatively normal.

I researched alternative pathways and found that Tibetan medicine, which has some similarity to traditional Indian and Ayurvedic medicine, suggests that disorders of movement in the legs is related to an imbalance of 'rLung' energy and that this rLung energy is connected to the mind and the nervous system. I worked out that of the three types of energies that Tibetan medicine states make up our constitution, mine was 48% rLung based. Further, the text by Dr Pema Dorjee, *Heal Your Spirit, Heal Yourself*, states that an imbalance of this energy is linked to the human states of desire and attachment.[20] There was definitely some truth in that but the knowledge was hardly something that could help me now. I decided that finding an authentic Tibetan medical doctor was not a path that I wished to follow at this point in time although it made for interesting reading.

No doubt there were other avenues of healing I could have explored but by this time I was getting quite frustrated with the range and depth of different approaches. Once again, researching the condition was becoming a cerebral activity. What did I really 'feel' about all of this? What really did work? I was totally lost in the opinions of others.

My restless legs and insomnia continued, sometimes better, sometimes worse. There seemed no rhyme or reason to it. I came to the point of giving up trying to work out what to do. There were too many conflicting opinions to digest and I couldn't decide what really was important or what worked for me.

So back to the meditation seat I went, where wisdom will occasionally sneak through into my conscious mind from some inner well of knowing. What came to me then, whilst sitting on my meditation cushion was an insight that my abdominal problems and my restless legs were linked. They both affected the lower half of my body and hadn't I always been a person to live in my head? My mind was always full of ideas and plans. In

20 Pema Dorjee, *Heal Your Spirit, Heal Yourself*, Watkins Publishing, London, 2005, p.162.

my younger years particularly, I was constantly moving, restless, an Aries. No wonder meditation felt like bliss. It was probably the only time that my mind and body were both still.

I wondered if both these conditions were caused by a blockage in the energy flow to the lower body chakras (subtle energy centres) and I started looking at ways to explore this possibility. I had long been aware of the flow of subtle energy in the body through my Tibetan meditation practices and to some extent through practicing qigong and tai chi. The ancient Chinese called this energy 'chi', the Indian sages called it 'prana' and the Tibetans referred to it as 'wind' made up of rlung, tripa and badkan. These cultures, and possibly many other ancient cultures, believe that if the channels or meridians through which the subtle energies flow remain clear and without obstruction, then this will lead to good energy flow to all the systems of the body and subsequently good health, both mental and physical.[21] These traditions have taught that we have other fields of energy around us that feed into our body but which we cannot see. Unfortunately, there are no scientific tests that can determine whether or not we have such blockages in our energy channels and such diagnoses tend to be subjective.

After my realisation that my problems may be associated with blocked lower body energy centres, the restless legs syndrome stopped. Vanished – just like that. I was dumbfounded. I had stopped using all of the suggested treatments in frustration and had had enough of trying to fix the problem. I couldn't believe it. Possibly in giving up, I was letting go. Letting go in Buddhism means not pushing, not trying to fix anything, not trying to control the outcome, accepting whatever comes with equanimity.

There is a wonderful passage called the *Six Words of Advice* from Tilopa (a Tibetan meditation master) and it goes like this:

21 Chuen, p.19.

'Let go of what has passed
Let go of what may come
Let go of what is happening now
Don't try to figure anything out
Don't try to make anything happen
Relax, right now, and rest.'[22]

Perhaps I had stumbled across the experience of this in stopping to search for a cure? Perhaps by operating under the intuition that my body/mind already had the answers to what was wrong with me and by meditating, I allowed that process to happen? By now also I was constantly aware of the title of this book – Digesting Life. It seemed to be floating in my consciousness.

I pondered that avoidance of life and its challenges could also mean that life remains 'undigested'. Undigested life energy gets blocked and is not able to flow to the lower body and its chakras. After this insight, I have been journeying along this path – learning about bringing the life force or energy down into the lower body – learning about grounding and centering the energy not just in meditation sessions but also through doing other practices throughout the whole day. It all comes back to the original concept of learning awareness of the body. I also realised that the lower energy centres are associated with the concept of being in the here and now – being present. Life is a journey and the learning never stops.

Origins and Effect of Disease

Understanding the origins of disease can assist our quest for awareness of our body. Disease and pain are multifactorial in origin and can be relieved or healed by multiple factors. Illness appears to be a product of complex factors: physical, environmental, genetic, dietary, radiation, emotional, mental and spiritual. Because we are a delicate mix of matter, mind and

22 K McLeod, *Wake up to Your Life*, Harper, San Francisco, 2002, p.223.

energy, our illness may originate from any (or all) of these levels and in different proportions.

Scientists now attribute disease to originating from gene expression, i.e. which genes in our makeup are switched on at a particular time and which genes are switched off. This activation appears to be related to both environmental factors and also to our perception of our environment. According to cellular biologist Bruce H. Lipton, how we perceive the world has an effect on our biological functions.[23] This is turn selects particular genes to make specific proteins to fit the environmental factors. If this is indeed the case, then our beliefs and our thoughts are prominent contributors to our health.

Many genetic mutations that cause genetic diseases are now understood and many diagnostic tests are now available to search for the presence of specific disease propensities. Scientists are attempting to trace the origins of disease and these include factors such as the biological (including genetic), maternal health, environmental, societal, psychological and emotional factors as causative.[24] There remains however, a huge variation in gene expression in the human form and there remains much that is still unknown about many forms of disease. It is interesting to see the progress in scientific research over the last ten years in searching for the origins of disease, particularly as scientists are now accepting the fact that the mind and emotions can play a causative part.

Although the mind is not usually the sole cause of a physical illness, it can, as we have seen above, play a part. The mind can apparently also be employed to affect the body specifically through the use of creative imagery and visualisation, as used in healing methods. Images and symbols are the earliest and most primitive part of mind and they affect the body on a very deep and

23 B H Lipton, *The Biology of Belief,* Hay House, USA, 2005.
24 C Hassed, *New Frontiers in Medicine,* Michelle Anderson Publishing, Melbourne, 2005, p.53.

primitive level. Ian Gawler, founder of the Gawler Foundation in Melbourne, has utilised and taught very successful healing work using creative imagery to assist people afflicted by cancer.[25] We know that thoughts not only affect emotions, moods, and impulses but also energy patterns in the body so we know that there is a subtle interchange always between mind and body.

Buddhists have the wonderful concept of 'karma' which links cause and effect and basically says that everything that happens has a cause even if we don't know what that cause is. To my mind this is quite a useful way to explain illness when we can't find a clear scientific explanation. Most of us do understand that life flows in patterns and often we don't see the benefit of misfortune until much time has passed. Indeed when we look back we see that things seem to always work out for the best, if not for the easiest and most direct route in life!

I am not suggesting that karma is the sole cause of our illness or disease. It is simply another aspect of its origin. Karma is the philosophy that our actions done intentionally have both long term and short term repercussions for us. An unhealthy lifestyle contributing to chronic disease is a type of immediate karma that is easy to see. To take this a little further, it is suggested that harming someone, for instance, can set up energetic repercussions that may take lifetimes to resolve. Buddhists believe that this negative build up of energy may contribute to illness and it is said that some karma may also come with us from previous lives. Karma is a good theory but when I am sick I really don't want to know that I am repaying old karma and to be thankful for that. When feeling unwell, it is quite difficult to act with decorum and thankfulness!

It is very important not to see illness as a penalty or punishment, but to see it as an opportunity to learn more about

---

25 I Gawler, *The Mind that Changes Everything*, Brolga Publishing, Melbourne, 2011, p.73.
I Gawler, *The Creative Power of Imagery*, Hill of Content, Melbourne, 1997.

our self-development through our reaction to the illness, while the illness takes its course. Illness then becomes a learning opportunity. Positive propensities are accumulated again by how we deal with our challenge or how we grow psychologically and emotionally through experiencing our illness. The system of karma is useful in that it encourages self-responsibility for our lives. There is no God who punishes or rewards; we are solely in charge of our own fate. Our motivation and attitudes NOW, determine our future. It is unfortunate that we are often ignorant of the part that we play in our fate.

Western medicine can save lives. Having worked in the acute hospital setting, I have seen this time and time again. Western medicine works well for acute illness and many less acute illnesses but as the level of urgency decreases, so the extent of what we can do to help ourselves increases. From the point of view of illness prevention, this is mostly up to us. If Western medicine can buy us time during acute and moderate illness to work on our deeper bodily and spiritual issues then we need to accept it. However, we also need to realise that medication and surgery are not the complete answer. There is much more to illness than that.

Disciplines like Traditional Chinese Medicine (TCM) explain illness in terms of patterns of imbalance, which is a more holistic way of looking at the body.[26] Imbalances in both the organs of the body and the chi (subtle energy) flow which connects them are considered to be the culprits of disease, so that treating only the head for a headache would be considered ridiculous in TCM. TCM uses herbs, meditative movement such as tai chi and qigong, acupuncture, living in accordance with the body's natural rhythms, dietary changes and shiatsu. It emphasises holistic care for the body, preventative care, and teaches that good health takes time to regain after illness. I am not advocating we all change from Western medicine to TCM but I do advocate

26 J Sauer, *The Perfect Day Plan*, Allen and Unwin, Australia, 2009.

becoming more informed about all the possible contributing factors of our illness.

The Lessons of Illness

The lesson of illness can be greater awareness. We learn through bitter experience that physical and mental illness really challenges our need to control. Illness can be slippery and elusive. One day we suffer, the next day it's gone, or changed in some way. One particular treatment helps for a while and then it doesn't anymore. One day we feel complete frustration and then all of a sudden the problem disappears. We really can't fathom the reasons a lot of the time.

Part of the lesson or gift of illness is to teach us to be patient and to go with the process rather than against it. In fact, if we can look on our illness as a process which has a purpose, rather than some external event that is happening to us, all the better. We are obliged to learn to be humble when the body fails us. Sometimes it requires us to let go of our strict routines, our rigid ideas, and our controlled ways of living. Often it forces us to stop what we're doing, to reflect, to reconsider and to change. It encourages us to have an open mind and to perhaps consider using methods we have some resistance to. Sometimes we may need to take those medicines that we'd rather not take. Sometimes we may just have to wait it out.

From another angle we know that illness causes suffering, whether it is simply inconvenience or severe disability, it is all suffering of some sort. By experiencing this type of suffering we become more tolerant and understanding of ourselves as well as others going through a similar process. We may even feel their pain as our own if we are close to that other suffering person. We may develop compassion for others. From our own side, it is important to remember the effect that our illness can have on others and to be responsible for dealing with our own suffering.

It is all too easy to transfer blame and responsibility for it to those around us. By learning to recognise when and how we do this, we begin to grow as a person.

A friend of mine tells me that when she is ill she accepts that she will just 'bumble along' for a while. In other words, she drops her usual expectations of that day and allows herself be less judgmental of herself. She tries to focus on what she can do rather than what she can't do and uses the feeling of gratitude for what she does have to help her through that day. If we allow ourselves to focus unrelentingly on our problems, our reality will become constricted to the point where we develop a mental tunnel vision. This is when we really suffer. Anything that helps us open to life again is useful.

Why Does Everything Seem to Happen at Once?

Why do some people seem to get one illness after another? I have often heard people say that 'it all happens at once', meaning that once one thing goes wrong with the body, other illnesses seem to present themselves. Sometimes this process can go on for years before a period of relative bodily health resumes.

My view is that it's all about internal balance and inter-dependence. The balance or imbalance in the energy systems and physical systems of the body affect each other. We obviously can't see what's going on in our body chemistry and physiology but it is often at this very tiny molecular and energetic level that the imbalance begins. There may be several causes for the imbalance and perhaps the body can cope with one or two but when there are five or six causes active at one time, the body exceeds its threshold of balance and starts to experience symptoms. By this stage the imbalance has been going on for quite some time but we have been unaware of it, due to the body's superb ability to compensate. Then, once one system is malfunctioning, the other systems are affected and we have a snowball effect, resulting in the feeling that everything is breaking down at once. Sometimes we need to work on one system at a time but generally we won't be well until all our systems are functioning and balanced, despite the symptoms of illness appearing to disappear. What we consider a mystery really just reflects the intricate balance between all the systems and organs of our body. Not being able to see them makes it a mystery. Biologists and scientists are still discovering new information about how the body functions. It seems a very complex machine indeed.

Still Some Mystery

Illness, or the symptoms of illness, come and go and as such are impermanent. They constantly change from moment to moment. The Tibetan physician, Dr Pema Dorjee, in *Heal Your Spirit, Heal Yourself* says that if we heal our spirit, we heal all of us and that the mind is the root of all suffering.[27] This is a tall order but one that is echoed throughout spiritual literature. What it is saying is that through working on the spiritual body (becoming more conscious, compassionate, wise and more able to view reality correctly), we will see a flow on effect in the health of our other 'bodies' such as the psychological, the emotional, the energetic and the physical. In my own life I have seen this concept working on a general level.

Accident, illness and injuries will continue to arise with an element of unpredictability, no matter how well we look after our bodies and no matter how wise we become. No one escapes illness and death. No matter how spiritually evolved we may be, our bodies remain impermanent, limited bodies. They can only do so much and last for so long. Considering all this then, it would be reasonable to state that we can improve and maintain good health up to a point if we also work on the spiritual or psychological, but that illness and death retain an element of unpredictability. There is still much that we don't know.

27 Dorjee, p.27

For now, we have awareness training to help us be vigilant as regards our health. People who have or who are suffering from illnesses such as cancers continually encourage people to be more aware of any changes happening in their bodies and they encourage people to take action and to have those changes examined by a professional before the disease progresses to the stage where treatment is too late. Awareness of body is advised as a tool for keeping healthy.

Pain

Pain can powerfully bring our awareness into the body. Chronic pain seems to achieve this more than a short-lived pain, the message of which is quickly forgotten. Pain which endures, even though it fluctuates, forces us to focus our attention on the body. Watching one's own behaviours when ill can be quite comical if we are able to detach and simply observe. We all handle pain differently but there is no doubt that pain requires us to learn how to manage pain.

Apart from medication or surgery, there are many avenues available to us when we explore how to deal with pain. From the point of view of spiritual work, particular meditation practices can be useful if the pain is not overwhelming. Various techniques include mindfulness practice, relaxing around the pain, distraction, compassion practices, visualisation or healing imagery and I have also found Buddhist Vajrayana/Tantric meditation to be useful. Many times I have been surprised to find that after finishing a meditation session, the migraine that was threatening has disappeared or the completely blocked hay fever nose has magically cleared. There have been stories of meditation masters being able to remove themselves from their body at will during severe pain. For most of us this is impossible but nevertheless, we can deduce that pain is definitely influenced by one's state of mind, something we all have experienced even in non-meditative situations.

Norman Doidge, a psychiatrist and psychoanalyst, in his book *The Brain That Changes Itself* states that "pain, like our body image is a construct of the brain" and the book contains an interesting discussion on the neurological mechanism of pain, especially the idea of 'brain maps' and learned pain.[28] He discusses that the brain, having the function of neuroplasticity, is capable of creating new circuits in response to pain which may then be difficult to change after a certain length of time, even when the original pain has passed. From this book we come to appreciate just how important the brain is in determining our response to pain. I have experienced and been intrigued by the fact that when I am in a situation where it is inappropriate to express a strong verbal response to a painful event, the pain is much more manageable than it would otherwise have been, or that I can bear it better. It seems that the experience of pain is a very complex interaction between body and mind. It is this ability of the mind to moderate pain that has been discovered by meditators over the centuries.

Stephen Levine brought pain meditations to the west with his book *A Gradual Awakening* written in the 1980s.[29] Buddhism teaches that pain is impermanent and a good focus for meditation. Steven Levine's meditations taught how to 'be' with the pain, how to observe it without trying to alter it and how to see that pain continually moves with regard to location, depth and intensity. He taught the art of relaxing into the pain. It seems that he was able to take this even a step further by adding visualisation techniques – indeed, he tells a story in which he was able to move a kidney stone and pass it out of his body by relaxing in a warm bath and visualising the stone moving out. It appears that some people are able to train their minds to relax with pain. Most of us fear pain and paradoxically, it is this fear and the resulting tension in the body which can intensify the pain even more.

28 Doidge, p.190
29 S Levine, *A Gradual Awakening*, Doubleday, New York, 1989, p.100

Body Image

No discussion of awareness of the body is complete without a mention of body image. Body image is part of one's overall self-image or self-concept so it is closely associated with awareness of self. Body image is defined as how you think, perceive and feel about your body. Body image at first glance may appear to be solely about our bodies however research has found that its basis includes genetic, psychological, neurological and behavioural causes.

In Western society, body image is perceived as the top personal concern of any 11-24 year old.[30] We also know that anorexia nervosa has the highest mortality rate of any psychiatric illness, with a death rate higher even than that of major depression.[31] Eating disorders are now thought to be a form of mental illness. This is not difficult to understand as so much of our eating behaviour tends to have an emotional component. Add to that our tendency towards food likes and dislikes and the availability of a huge choice in food globally and the web of eating behaviour becomes very complex.

When we look at how we develop a sense of our own body and its relationship to what is around us, we are told that it arises from two main sources, both of which are equally powerful. One is that body image arises from what we are told as we are growing up. Increasingly advertising is playing a large part in that component. The second source is our own physiological brain development which ensures that we develop a sense of ourselves as an entity having personal boundaries and a spatial sense of our body existing. This particular sense develops through sight, proprioception and balance and requires normal

30 Mission Australia's National Survey of Young Australians, 2010, retrieved 15 October 2010, <http://www.indymedia.org.au>
31 Independent Media Centre of Australia, *Fighting for Positive Body Image for Young Women*, retrieved 15 Nov 2011,< http://www.indymedia.org.au/2011/02/15/fighting-for-positive-body-image-for-young-women

physiological/neuronal development.[32] Both of these origins of our body image arise in the brain.

Additionally, behavioural causes for our self-image may involve critical messages or abuse from our family members during childhood which may have caused us to see ourselves negatively. Ongoing abuse may teach us to become passive in life or even to feel a victim in many life situations. In a similar way there may have been other negative pressures on us originating at work or at school. Body image then arises from a combination of factors. Included in this whole process is not only how we see ourselves but also how we think others see us. Many women have been taught that 'looking nice' is expected and necessary if we are to be loved. Our self-image is very much bound up in how the body looks.

Looking at body image as it relates to beauty, we see that society has always favoured beauty and this has resulted in more advantages for those possessing a good physique and a pleasant face. This stereotype or evolutionary pattern ensures that handsome or beautiful people tend to be more popular, get better jobs, get better looking partners, and are even seen to possess desirable qualities such as goodness, intelligence and trustworthiness. In our modern Western society, advertising has made it impossible to avoid being continually shown what society supposedly values with regard to appearance and body shape – and these standards are unrealistically high.

This has had a detrimental affect which has been particularly powerful in the last two generations of people. If we look closely at beautiful people and how they feel about themselves we see that mostly they too are insecure about their appearance, they may have low-self esteem despite being attractive and they feel pressure to continue to look attractive. Cosmetic surgery is a

32 P Larsen & I Lubkin, '*Body Image*', *in 7th edit. Chronic Illness: Impact and Intervention*, Jones and Bartlett, Massachusetts, 2009, pp. 117-138.

profession based solely on this societal influence and it appears that women are much more likely to see their bodies negatively than men do. It is quite possible that an archetypal pattern has emerged in women over thousands of years, making them feel that they must look attractive in order to be desired and therefore for them to survive. We see then a huge societal influence in our self-concept and body image and many of us internalise societal standards. It takes a mentally strong individual to reject these standards as unrealistic.

Mood also plays a role in how we experience our bodies. A person with a low mood or depression tends to extend their negative thinking to include his/her body image and this includes the distortion of how they see their bodies. Eating a supposedly 'bad' high-calorie food may be enough to alter how a person sees the body after the snack, as opposed to before eating it. The brain is such a powerful instrument and it is so important that we acquaint ourselves with how it works. Sometimes our own brain interprets things to our detriment. Our self-image is a mental picture that we have of ourselves and this mental picture can be very resistant to change, often having accumulated over many years of criticism or other unfavourable experiences during our childhood.

Poor body image is a difficult and complex area to understand and statistically it is not an easy area to treat when things go wrong. The issue of body image goes deep. Its roots are in the mind. Its secrets, if we want to unravel them, come from the part of our psyches which are not conscious, at least at the beginning. By focusing our awareness on our body during meditation or even with cognitive skills in counselling, we still often battle with how to change our perception of ourselves because this perception involves deep emotional roots and neurological pathways. These neuronal circuits can be very persistent and difficult to change even when people become aware of them. Many women recognise that comfort or binge eating is associated with depression or a feeling of powerlessness. The triggers for the depression may be a perceived inability to plan future events, to be certain about an outcome (emotionally safe) or to have personal control in a situation. To go deeply and with awareness into these feelings can be confronting and even then we may be left with 'living with' our weaknesses rather than curing or completely eliminating them.

Jungian dream analysis is an excellent therapy which allows us to work with these deep emotions and fears, bringing the roots of these patterns into our consciousness so that we truly look at them directly. Jungian dream analysis (named after its founder Carl Gustav Jung), which deals with uncovering areas of un-awareness in our psyche, can help us to see that our own tight control on how we appear externally to others is currently self-imposed. Although in the past we may have interpreted signals from society, family or others to mean that we must be a particular way to be accepted, in the present time nobody else has these expectations of us. Our dreams can actually show us where these judgements originate from, often going back to events which happened many years ago. Every little emotional memory is stored deep within the unconscious.

Awareness of body, as with so many other life issues, is not always something we can work on using a conscious level of mind. Meditation will help develop conscious awareness of the mental aspect, illness and injury will help develop awareness of the physical aspect, as will dance, tai chi or body work. But there is another part of body awareness that remains deeply unconscious and we may need professional psychotherapeutic help to access that deep, psychological aspect of body awareness.

Western psychotherapy is beginning to incorporate a Buddhist concept which says that we need to connect and stay with our deep feelings and emotions in order to heal.[33] This is

33 Z Segal, J Williams & J Teasdale, *Mindfulness-Based Cognitive Therapy for Depression*, The Guilford Press, New York, 2002.

called 'mindfulness' practice and it involves just being with an emotion or feeling without avoiding it and without analysing it. It involves contacting a very calm state of mind in which we are aware of thoughts and emotions passing through the mind and yet we allow these thoughts to be present without trying to influence them in any way. This technique creates a 'distance' or objectivity between us and our feelings and as a consequence we don't feel overpowered by them while we observe them. This technique done repeatedly is said to loosen the bonds that these thought patterns have over us, however this process may take some time and is not to be rushed. We may have an immense fear of staying with difficult emotions and the process must be done with great sensitivity.

Our body image may change over time through learning about gender differences and roles, through performing a job or sport, through childbearing and relationships, through changes in body and brain chemistry and through illness and aging. Chronic illness and physical accidents particularly can modify our body image or bring to our attention what our self-concept is. [34]

We have several choices: we can try to meet society's ideal body image, we can adjust the ideal to fit our own situation, we can reject the ideal body image, or we can simply be aware of what is going on in our minds as regards our body image. How we work with this continual adjustment is a lifelong process. What is quite clear is that the mind is hugely influential in how we see ourselves and our bodies. Even if we are unable to eradicate these patterns of thought because they are so persistent and stubborn, simply being aware of them and not judging ourselves for having them, will create a more spacious and accepting awareness in our lives.

34 Larsen & Lubkin, pp. 117-138.

Awareness of Subtle Energy in the Body

Meditation, tai chi, yoga, martial arts and qigong are disciplines which can help us to feel and move the energy along the subtle energy channels or meridians of the body. These energy channels are not visible and are not able to be seen with a microscope but we can sense them within our bodies and we can sense shifts in our subtle energy if we pay attention. As we know, the body has an electromagnetic field. It also has chemical energy within its cells and systems which fire many physiological functions by causing heat, movement, digestion, nerve impulses, hormonal circuits and more. Reading a text on body physiology is a fascinating read. It is difficult for us to feel the body's inner workings; however it is possible to become aware of the energy patterns in the body and surrounding it. We will discuss awareness of subtle energy in more detail in chapter six.

* * *

Recently I was forced back into a time of self-reflection by an episode of acute back pain. Lying horizontal on my bed for several days, I saw very clearly how I continue to go through life focused on the future. I have not yet learned to be present in each moment with gratitude, presence and consideration. The body's ailments are tools which teach me that I have more to learn. In this way, the body can be looked upon as a teacher. It pulls us up and shows us what we forget to notice.

A final great benefit of illness is learning about letting go of expectations, control and desire for things to be perfect. It is very necessary when we have done all that we can to heal, to then step back, let go and allow the process of illness to run its course. Without this final deep letting go and acceptance, all the will in the world will not bring about lasting change and good health. When we get to that point of surrendering control, then somehow the deep patterns slowly begin to loosen and we feel a shift. I have seen this happen time and time again. Of course healing is possible even without physical healing occurring. We can still experience mental, psychological and spiritual healing, despite our bodies being imperfect. A physical illness does not prevent growth on other levels. We can continue to heal relationships and love others concurrently with physical illness. It is only in life's most challenging moments, when all appears to be lost through misfortune, illness or death, that we finally realise the only truly important thing in life, is love.

CHAPTER FOUR
AWARENESS OF MIND

The Mind and Suffering

We often first become aware of our mind and curious about its workings when we begin to notice that our thoughts are negative or unhelpful. In fact, we may even notice that our thoughts seem to prolong and intensify our suffering over life's misfortunes. Most of us will experience grief and loss in various forms in this lifetime but each person will have a different way of dealing with these. When we come to the point of being interested in what is happening in our minds during and after stressful events, we have already achieved a huge step forward towards becoming more aware human beings.

Mental and Emotional Suffering

Mental and emotional suffering can be of different degrees for different people depending on the circumstances and on the personality. Some people experience only mild emotional and mental stress and others go on to develop what is called 'mental illness'. The irony is that the more we suffer, the greater the potential can be to change ourselves, providing of course that we determine to find a way out of our suffering.

Oliver Sacks in his book *Awakenings*[35] quotes Nietzsche as saying:

> 'Only great pain, the long, slow pain that takes it's time... compels us to descend to our ultimate depths... I doubt that such pain makes us 'better'; but I know it makes us more profound... In the end, in case what is most important remain unsaid: from such abysses, from such severe sickness, one returns newborn, having shed one's skin... with merrier senses, with a second dangerous innocence in joy, more childlike and yet a hundred times subtler than one has ever been before.'

For Oliver Sacks the whole message of his book is embedded in the title *Awakenings*, which is another way of saying 'becoming more aware'. Incidentally, the Buddhist term for becoming fully aware is 'enlightenment'.

More recently authors D'Aquili and Newberg[36] have a neuroscientific theory to explain why it is that we can learn so much from deep emotional pain. They state that during 'increased emotional discharge especially when associated with a high emotional state' there is 'a certain degree of neural instability, allowing for the formation of new connections between neurons.' Others such as neurologist Norman Doidge support a similar scientific view that the brain is indeed capable of continual change in response to new experiences.[37]

35 O Sacks, *Awakenings*, Picador, London, 1991, p.289.
36 D'Aquili & Newberg, p.161
37 Doidge, p.26

In the last twenty years there has been increasing media, government and medical interest in psychology and mental illness. There has also been a mushrooming of therapies, treatments and medications to help deal with this increasing problem. When I began to investigate the origin of my mental suffering I stumbled across Buddhism, as Buddhism has much to say on this topic of developing awareness of mind. In fact Buddhism proposes that awareness of mind, along with awareness of body, feelings and phenomena, lead to greater contentment, self-understanding and peace of mind.[38]

No doubt other religions and philosophies have helped many others develop insight into this problem of mental suffering/ illness. Because of the Western culture that I live in, I was encouraged to use Western treatments such as medication, counselling and psychotherapy. At the same time I also carried out an investigation of how the mind operates according to Eastern religions. My path has continued to pick the most effective from several Eastern and Western systems, gradually fine tuning my approach over the years to what really works for me.

We now live such global lives, that our psyches are also beginning to embrace different cultural approaches to a global human problem. Global consciousness is emerging and our lives are beginning to reflect that. I feel that it is possible to use self-development practices from different traditions during the course of our search for wholeness. While the effects of a practice may be slightly different when practiced by someone from a different cultural background, nevertheless benefits often emerge.

38 L Rosenberg, *Breath by Breath – The Liberating Practice of Insight Meditation*. Shambhala, Boston, 1999.

What is the Mind?

It is important to remember that in any discussion of our mind we need to have some understanding of what the mind actually is. Western scientists have tended to assume that the mind is encased in the brain but throughout cultures and traditions this idea varies. There are many theories and attempted definitions but no theory which everyone agrees on. While we know much about the human brain, scientifically we know little about the mind. People who have investigated the mind, mostly meditators or spiritual practitioners, have done so experientially and have explained their experiences of mind in terms which mean little to others who have not had these experiences. On the other hand, Western scientists, who follow a strictly defined scientific method when determining the validity of anything, find it difficult to pinpoint what the mind is.

Two Aspects of Mind

In the Eastern spiritual traditions it is said that there are two aspects of mind. One aspect is the conceptual, analytical, 'thinking mind' which is housed in the brain, and the other is 'natural mind', which is a mind state experienced when the conceptual mind rests. Our thinking mind is easy enough to experience and understand, but just the same, we can be completely unaware of how it operates whilst we are immersed in our moment to moment experience. Natural mind proves to be a little more elusive in terms of experiencing and defining. Natural mind is noted to be the mind which is present as a constant and stable background to the everyday, problem-solving conceptual mind. It is a bit like the clear sky ever present behind the clouds. It is said to be empty yet to contain a potentiality.

Furthermore, this natural mind is said to be the basis of positive qualities such as peace, bliss, wisdom and compassion and to complicate matters even further, it is said to be boundaryless – so it is not confined to any particular area. Another main quality that natural mind is said to contain is pure awareness or clarity.

The great Tibetan meditation master Kalu Rinpoche[39] discusses natural mind and explains that in this experience (of the natural mind) is the seed or the potential for full awakening. Buddhism encourages us to develop awareness of both of these mind states, conceptual mind and natural mind, and has produced much literature and many experiential practices to help us with this.

Many texts have been written on the natural mind by philosophers and spiritual people and it can be confusing when we begin to investigate our mind and the role it plays in our happiness. My sense is that mind is experienced on different levels, some quite easily detected with practice (such as thoughts), some more subtle and perhaps unconscious (such as emotions and dreams), some more subtle still (moments of absolute mental stillness, stability and peace) and some exceedingly subtle (such as natural mind).

I have found it imperative to learn how to balance the thinking mind, which has the ability to become restless even tormenting, with the clear natural mind, which brings great peace. In our society it is very easy to lose the capacity for quiet contemplation and reflection. Continual exposure to the internet, computers, mobile phones and other technology, keeps our minds perpetually racing. People now are being rewarded for having a scattered mind, a mind that can flit from one thing to another and skim material at surface level in record speed. This comes at the loss of our ability to slow and focus our mind. Our brain naturally wants to be distracted. It wants to know everything. Heading off in the direction of restlessness and continual thinking needs to be balanced by periods of rest, mindless physical activity,

39 Kalu Rinpoche, *Gently Whispered*, Station Hill Press, New York, 1994, p.22

focusing on one thing only or stillness.

We have so far discussed briefly the two states of mind called conceptual mind and natural mind. There are other states of mind or states of consciousness such as sleep, dream and the unconscious mind, transitional states between waking and sleeping, dying and deep meditation. For the scope of this book I will confine the discussion to the two mind states most useful and important to us if we want to embark on the path of meditation: the conceptual or thinking mind and natural mind.

Some meditation or therapeutic practices work specifically on conceptual mind – for example, cognitive behavioural therapy, working with imagery, affirmations, dream work and mindfulness based meditations. Some practices work on natural mind – for example, becoming 'lost' in the beauty of nature or other moments when time seems to stop still, and the Dzogchen and Mahamudra meditation practices of Buddhism. Then there are practices which may work on either mind states or both, depending on the experience of the practitioner – for example, breath meditation practices and the esoteric Tantric/Vajrayana meditation practices of Tibet. I have tried many of these practices and have found something useful in all of them. Many I continue with to this day. The main point is to find practices or therapies which teach us awareness and how to balance both of these states of mind: the conceptual, thinking mind and the natural, still mind.

I unashamedly advocate for meditation (along with other therapies which may be used concurrently) as the practice most able to bring about mental balance. It is particularly useful for people with overactive conceptual minds. For many reasons, anxiety and depression are becoming more common in society today. These behaviours are basically learned patterns of reacting to life's events and they can definitely be modified by the practice of meditation. If we resolve to become aware of our mind-stream during the day we will soon notice these blind repetitive patterns happening again and again, almost unconsciously. These are the patterns which cause us so much suffering and unhappiness. In my life, meditation has helped me immensely to become more aware of these patterns and to modify them.

The Practice of Meditation

Buddhist meditation is changing form in our Western society and it is possible to have many of the benefits of this ancient tradition without changing our cultural heritage and lifestyle. Many readers of this book will not be Buddhist and I include myself in that category. What I have found however, is that by using the practices of Buddhism, we naturally learn much of the philosophy and this does change the way we live our lives. Similar to any other form of education, new knowledge and experiences will change us. Meditation is a choice and may not resonate with all people. As it has touched my life very deeply for the better, I encourage others to try it and I have taught it to many people in a non-religious way with sometimes quite profound effects.

The techniques of meditation involve practices which:

- Teach us how to relax the body and calm the mind.
- Encourage us to observe the workings of our conceptual mind and the world in which we live, resulting in greater awareness.
- Teach us to focus our mind and be more present in the present moment.
- Train us to quieten and still the thinking mind, leading to mental stillness, greater clarity, insight and wisdom.
- Lead us toward the experience of a natural, still mind, showing us the true mind free of all our attitudes, beliefs, ego and fears.
- Give us experiences of qualities such as love, compassion, joy and balance.

- May give us mystical experiences such as union, loss of self and connection with the divine.
- May lead to experiences of how our subtle energy flows in our body.

How Does Meditation Work?

Brain chemistry

Essentially, with the practice of meditation, we are changing the way we use our mind. We rest it, focus it, it slows, it stills – and then we notice what happens in the mind, the body and the inner energies as we remain in that still state. As this is a mental process, different experiences constantly arise. We train our minds to be still and this alters our brain chemistry or neurophysiology. There are definitely neurophysiological mechanisms which arise in the brain as we meditate.[40] Western studies of long term meditators show that meditation produces profound changes in the brain.[41] As a result, the chemical balance in the whole body changes, bringing about greater wellbeing. For many people, positive qualities, particularly love and wellbeing, are often noted to arise from the repeated practice of meditation, whether it is religious or not.

Active and Passive

The practice of meditation requires being able to balance active and passive aspects of the mind. To explain: it is now known that the two hemispheres of the brain each have their own interpretation of the world that we live in and that it is necessary that we have both of these versions so that the end result or view is a more complete one.[42] Information which we receive from the left hemisphere tends to be rational, focused and specific,

40 D'Aquili & Newberg, p.110
41 State Government of Victoria, Better Health Channel, *Fact sheet: Meditation*, retrieved 8 June 2011, <http://www.betterhealth.vic.gov.au/bhcv2/bhcarticles.nsf/pages/Meditation
42 See McGilchrist.

whereas information from the right hemisphere tends to be broader, richer, and more interconnected, and its view searches beyond what the mind can currently experience. Of course both of these parts of the brain are connected and every function of the brain is carried out by both. The left hemisphere, however, has more of the function of focus or concentration and the right hemisphere has more of the function of a spacious, more open awareness. In our more primitive days we required both of these abilities so that we could concentrate on hunting prey whilst simultaneously being aware of any dangers around us.

In most meditative techniques we use both of these functions – we use concentration, focus or mindfulness and then we alternate that with a more open spacious awareness. Often we learn concentration first and then go on to develop the spacious awareness until one day we find that they arise simultaneously.

Subtle Energy

Meditation also has an important effect on one's subtle energy (also sometimes called chi or prana). Subtle energy is linked with our state of mind. As a result of going deeply in meditation, we may experience shifts or changes in our inner subtle energy and as a result we feel more balanced in both body and mind after meditation. The Dalai Lama goes some way towards explaining this when he says that mind, consciousness, matter and prana (subtle energy) are essentially the same. "At the most fundamental level, no absolute division can be made between mind and matter. In its subtlest form it is prana, a vital energy which is inseparable from consciousness."[43]

What affects any one of these things, affects them all. We are already aware of the mind/body connection – now we are becoming aware, through quantum physics and great spiritual sages of the past that we can influence all by working on one.

43 Dalai Lama, *The Universe in a Single Atom*, Broadway Books, New York, 2005, p.110

Meditation is a very powerful daily method of bringing body, mind and energy back into balance.

The Benefits of Meditation

Whether we use no technique (which can be more difficult for active minds) or choose one of the thousands of techniques available to us, the end result is the same. The most marked mental changes that we notice are that after meditation we experience increased levels of wellbeing, balance, awareness and kindness.[44] Meditation masters say that this is because we access the source of these qualities from coming into contact with natural mind[45] whereas scientists state that it is because the techniques alter our brain neurophysiology.[46] There is also ample evidence that meditation can assist a body to heal physically.[47] It doesn't really matter how meditation works – the truth is that with regular practice, it makes us feel much happier, more loving, think more positively and act more ethically.

The benefits of mindfulness and awareness practice are huge. Increasing one's self awareness is really a heightened consciousness of how we are in the world. We begin to see that how we are. We also begin to notice how we affect the environment, the planet, animals, matter – how connected everything is to everything else. We experience interdependence.

How Do We Meditate?

Meditation is quite simple. There is nothing difficult about it. Generally it is a good idea to begin by going to a teacher, a class, or listening to a CD, so that we can experience a guided meditation first. It may be harder to learn from a book or by

44 State Government of Victoria, Fact sheet.
45 Tenzin Wangyal Rinpoche, *Tibetan Sound Healing*, Sounds True, Boulder Colorado, 2011, p.5.
46 D'Aquili & Newberg, p.30.
47 I Gawler, *You Can Conquer Cancer*, Michelle Anderson Pu blishing, Melbourne, 2001.

oneself (but not impossible!). The simplest way to begin is to sit with a straight back in a relaxed way with the eyes closed, be still and notice what arises in the mind, notice the breath as it flows in and out, notice the sensations in the body, even the sounds around you, and just be with whatever arises. The idea is not to let the mind create stories about what is happening but to be aware of them and then allow them to pass. When the mind wanders away from this focus and we find ourselves thinking about something totally unrelated to the meditation, simply return again to the focus of the meditation. Meditation has been called mind training and we soon see why. Gradually the mind will settle, the breath will settle and the body will relax. This can be surprisingly difficult to do without some guidance as we are so used to being mentally busy. The idea of sitting still and doing nothing can be quite a foreign concept for us and the mind may flit from one thought to another. Therefore I teach people with guided meditations until they learn, with practice, to do these techniques by themselves.

One thing we soon notice is that if we can't relax the body then we can't relax the mind and it is worthwhile enlisting some help in learning relaxation techniques. Relaxation is the beginning of the process of meditation. Sometimes relaxation results in us going to sleep however, meditation occurs when we calm the mind without going to sleep. In fact, we need to be quite awake and aware to meditate because we are interested in observing the mind. Sometimes quite interesting experiences will arise as we sit in unaccustomed quiet and these early experiences often make us curious enough to continue. If we are lucky these early attempts at meditation will also bring mental peace and stillness, something to be highly prized in our rushed and busy world.

For those wishing specific advice on how to begin meditation I provide some general guidelines at the end of this chapter.

Which Technique to Use?

There are many techniques to choose from. We will find some easier to use than others, depending on our personality, life experiences and belief system and it may be necessary for us to experiment with a few different types of meditation before we find something that suits us and that we would be happy practicing for a reasonable period of time on a regular basis.

Body Relaxation Practices

This is a starting point for most people who learn to meditate. Relaxing the body is excellent for introducing us to the feelings of a rested body and a calm mind. We can use this practice to develop awareness of the body while in the meditation session. We will soon begin to notice that calming the body also calms the mind and so we learn about the mind/body interaction. For many people this type of meditation is sufficient. Going further involves a certain amount of trust and belief in meditation and also a willingness to invest a fair amount of time practicing it. Meditation teacher, author, veterinarian and founder of the Gawler Foundation for holistic cancer care, Ian Gawler, has shown the profound physical healing that can occur as a result of this type of body relaxation/mindfulness/stillness meditation.[48] The benefits are enormous for physical healing because learning how to put the body in a deep state of rest is, in effect, similar to allowing the body to sleep. It is a time when the body can regenerate and heal itself.

For those who wish to try a simple 10 minute body-relaxation meditation, suitable to begin with, I have included one in Appendix B at the conclusion of this book.

48 The Gawler Foundation, *Cancer and Mind Body Research*, retrieved 16 November 2011, <http:www. gawler.org/cancer-and-mind-body-research/>

Breath Meditation

Meditation which encourages us to be calm, quiet and stable is called stabilising meditation. It uses focus and concentration. Breath meditation is one of these techniques and is used in many different traditions. This type of meditation usually begins with observing the sensations of the breath (and the body as it breathes), not with our eyes but with our 'mind's eye'. I find it works better to only half focus on the breath and half focus on the sensations of the body as this leads to a more relaxed focus overall. There is no striving or forcing in meditation. In fact, if we do that, we will soon see that it is counterproductive. Traditional breath meditation usually won't be effective if we just sit for ten minutes a day, as it takes the mind a little longer to stabilize. Such meditations require us to begin with a short session and gradually extend the time. We can, however, use simple breath techniques, such as consciously lengthening and slowing the out-breath, to bring about a quick form of relaxation. There are Western adaptations to traditional practices which can be quite useful.

For those who wish to try a simple 20 minute breath meditation, I have included one in Appendix C at the end of this book.

Movement Meditation

Movement meditations such as yoga, walking meditations, qigong, tai chi and martial arts are also a good starting point for many people, especially those who find it difficult to sit still in meditation. During movement meditations we learn to focus on each specific movement of the body. This becomes the focus for the meditation. If we lose our place in the sequence of movements through becoming distracted, we soon know become aware of this, and we learn how to keep our focus on one thing only. This is a valuable lesson. These meditations bring an experience of mental calm just like sitting meditations.

Mindfulness Meditation

Mindfulness meditation is a meditation where we simply keep our attention on whatever it is we are doing in a deliberate way without mental judgement. For instance, we can be washing the dishes, driving the car, or taking a shower, while keeping our attention focused only on what we are experiencing and doing. We attempt to learn this skill with all types of meditation but it may be the most difficult thing we ever attempt to learn because our mind has a habit of moving on to the next issue or task whilst we are still doing the present task. This method can be practiced both during a sitting practice and during the day and has many benefits for developing more calm and less stress. I highly recommend a little book called *Take Your Time*[49] by Eknath Easwaran. It addresses simple ways to bring greater enjoyment, calm, mindfulness, and consideration for others into our daily lives.

Awareness Practice

This is essentially an extension of mindfulness practice. For example, I can be mindful of where I am putting my fingers on the keyboard to type this text and also simultaneously, I can be aware of the paragraph as a whole and how my present word is fitting into the whole sentence. So mindfulness of the present moment and awareness of the place of the present moment in the whole picture, happen together. They happen when we choose to stay focused on something. If our mind drifts off to something else then we are not being mindful. Another example is while practicing tai chi or a dance – while we are mindful of a particular movement that we are doing and its intricacies, we are also aware of where in the set/dance this movement is. The trick is to focus on one thing (mindfulness) and at the same time keep noticing other phenomena arising and passing away without allowing the mind to attach to them (this is awareness).

49 E Easwaran, *Take Your Time*, Nilgiri Press, California, 2008.

Mindfulness/awareness really means to pay attention and this can refer to experiences, thoughts, emotions and body sensations – anything really. It is a balancing act in a relaxed way. We are required to 'let go' of control, while simultaneously bringing our attention to the object of focus. Quite a skill!

The effect of this is that it allows our mind to observe itself without being disturbed by the phenomena passing through. By noticing and observing, especially mental states, we become aware of ourself. And by becoming aware repeatedly, we are able to change. It is very helpful to be able to remain aware of ourselves when we are in the midst of turbulent emotions because this quality of awareness brings more spaciousness to the situation and enables us to recognise that we have a choice in our reaction.

Insight Meditation

Once mental stability is established there will be a natural progression towards deepening our meditation, particularly with the breath practices. Breath practices over time lead to insight meditation, a practice which occurs when the mind really settles into stillness and we directly experience a new way of seeing reality. It is as though we see something familiar for the first time, we know or we have an insight into how things really are. Joseph Goldstein in *Insight Meditation*[50] explains this type of breath meditation rather well. We do need the thinking mind to be quite still for this experience however, which takes a little practice as our natural tendency is to go to sleep. If we can remain in this still state of mind we will begin to observe how the mind works and we may have spontaneous insights about all sorts of things we didn't realise before. Meditation is quite unique in that by doing absolutely nothing we can learn a lot!

50 J Goldstein, *Insight Meditation*, Shambhala, Boston, 1994, p.53.

Sound Meditations: Mantra-Chanting

The use of sound – such as mantra, chanting, or simply focusing on the sounds around us as we sit to meditate, can be highly effective. A simple modern awareness of sound meditation could be to sit outside, relax the body, close our eyes and listen to the sounds that we hear (the wind, the rain, the birds, the cars). We simply keep our attention gently focused on their coming and going without creating mental stories about the sounds. We listen for the pure sound without any mental analysis. If the mind wanders away from the sounds as it invariably will, we gently bring it back. Listening to the sound of a gong and following the sound with our full attention to the very end can also bring us very quickly into a state of stillness.

Mantra works by causing vibration which alters our internal energy and this in turn alters our state of mind. The mantra, when repeated for long enough, will amazingly cut through any mental chatter and we are left with an experience of 'natural mind' due to the dissolving of the conceptual mind. It is used extensively in Tibetan Buddhist meditation. Mantra work can be a difficult concept for our Western minds to comprehend unless we experience its affect for ourselves. The vibration of the sound while saying the mantra, vibrating in a specific area, affects the energy pathways of the subtle body. Perhaps also that repetitive sound stimulates a certain area of the brain, so contributing to the effect of the sound on the body and mind. It is possible to feel that the subtle energy in the body has shifted after doing mantra meditation work.

In the Tibetan Bon tradition we learn that it is also possible to arrive at the experience of natural mind through the use of sound. Tenzin Wangyal Rinpoche in *Tibetan Sound Healing* teaches a simple method that utilises singing seed syllables (certain sounds) which have the power to bring us deeply into our essence, very quickly.[51] These sounds are said to affect our internal energy through particular energy centres. This is another way to experience natural mind and is free of the trappings of traditional religion.

Contemplation

There is a more reflective type of meditation that involves reading a text, perhaps repeatedly and contemplating its meaning for a reasonable period of time. Religions often use this type of meditation. Buddhist contemplative meditations in particular have many levels of techniques to suit the beginner up to the advanced meditator but they all emphasise developing through contemplation and prayer the qualities of love, loving kindness, compassion, wisdom and balance (equanimity). As a Western meditation, the same principle of contemplation can be used to contemplate an issue in our lives during meditation when we are looking for an answer.

Visualisation

Visualisation is another technique sometimes incorporated into other meditations and sometimes used as a technique on its own. The practice of Buddhist Tantra (Vajrayana) uses visualisation along with mantra very effectively. Visualisation gives the mind something positive to focus on and the qualities associated with the deity or figure visualised are said to be absorbed into our own consciousness over time. In modern times visualisation has been used to achieve goals, manifest what we want and supposedly even to heal. Ian Gawler uses healing imagery exercises which appear to have marked physical and emotional healing capacities with some people.[52]

51 Tenzin Wangyal, *Tibetan Sound*, p. 5.
52 I Gawler, *The Mind That Changes Everything*, Brolga Publishing, Melbourne, 2011, p.115.

A Word About Mystical Experiences

We do not usually practice our meditation for this purpose however it is useful to know that sometimes higher meditative states or mystical experiences may arise.

A mystical experience is one form of a state of altered or heightened consciousness typically associated with certain religious, ritual, shamanistic or esoteric practices.

Mystical experiences arising from meditation include states such as bliss, ecstasy, peace, awe, absolute unity, connection with the divine/God/universal mind, and a dissolving of the boundaries of the self.

Modern neurotheologians D'Aquili and Newberg in *The Mystical Mind* have a scientific explanation for these experiences. They propose that religions often use the techniques such as repetition of texts or liturgy, devotion, mantra or repetitive prayer and ritual.[53] They say that these techniques alter which parts of our brain are active or stimulated at a particular time and over many thousands of years, religious people have perfected which practices lead to mystical experiences (or experiences of the divine).[54]

Mystical experience is uncommon in the general population and as yet not acknowledged by the Western scientific world, discussing them with people who are not open to them may not achieve anything unless they are a spiritual friend or have some understanding of these experiences. If such an experience does occur, we simply observe it arise and then pass away, as with any other experience.

53 D'Aquili & Newberg, p.91.
54 D'Aquili & Newberg, p.5.

Keep it Simple

It is not necessary to use complicated meditations or systems however, as we discover after much practice the simplest methods often work the best. A good general rule is initially to work on developing mental stability and body relaxation with a simple practice. A body-breath meditation is a wonderful way to do this although it would seem that whatever we are drawn to is a good place to start and in our Western society this would include working on our ego structure alongside meditation practices. Psychotherapy in any of its forms is appropriate work for most people who aspire to do inner work, as meditation alone will usually not transform or remove all our old ego patterns.

What About Awareness of Feelings and Emotions?

Emotions are strong energy forms which will not be denied. According to Matthieu Ricard in his book *Happiness* the word emotion comes from the Latin verb 'emovere' which means 'to move'.[55] Emotions then can be thought of as capable of moving the mind. Emotions and feelings are an integral part of our human experience, being complex systems, deeply embedded in our individual and collective psyches. They are often unconscious responses and a significant part of our inner work will be spent in trying to understand them. If we observe our emotions, we see the involvement of both physical responses (body) and cognition (mind). William Tiller, a scientist, states rather boldly that emotions are the informational molecular links between body and mind.[56] Much scientific research is now in progress on the link between our emotions and our DNA.

In the Buddhist tradition emotions are said to be closely related to thoughts. In fact, the two cannot be separated. Modern science has verified this by discovering that every part of the brain

---

55 M Ricard, *Happiness: A Guide to Developing Life's Most Important Skill,* Atlantic Books, London. 2007.
56 W Tiller, *Conscious Acts of Creation,* the Emergence of a New Physics, Pavior Pub, California, 2001.

that has been found to be associated with an emotion has also been found to have a cognitive aspect.[57] Buddhism's traditional teachings focused on cultivating positive mental states and this was emphasized as the method for overcoming negative thoughts and emotions. Courage, compassion and mental stability were highly regarded whereas negative characteristics were seldom mentioned. Mental illness and by association negative emotions were rarely mentioned in the texts, perhaps because this reflected the culture of the countries where these teachings originated.

Much work has been done by philosophers over the years in attempting to determine the origin of emotions and more recently there is a renewed interest in examining them. We know that emotions are influenced by our state of mind and are closely tied in with our judgements about a situation. Researchers state that fear is our most basic and primitive emotion and that emotion is a characteristic that has helped humans to learn quickly and so to aid our survival as a species.[58] A situation which results in serious pain or injury soon teaches us to avoid that situation next time. Unfortunately this type of quick learning has resulted in response behaviours becoming deeply embedded in our collective psyche. We notice the strength of this response particularly when we are confronted with a person who looks markedly different to us or when we are surprised by a snake on our path.

Not is all lost however. Over time, the human brain has developed the ability to think in more complex ways. It has also developed the ability to be more aware of itself. For instance, the primitive response of fear to something different in its environment (which may have been interpreted as a threat by primitive man) can now be partly overridden by cognitive reasoning. It is possible to develop the ability of partly altering our response if we recognize that the stimulus in our environment is no longer life threatening. For many of us this skill in becoming

57 Le Doux, p.21.
58 Le Doux, p. 131.

more aware of our often deep seated and emotional responses can have a marked result on how we interact with others – especially those who are different. Moderating emotions before we act them out and possibly harm ourselves or others, is a growing body of knowledge.

When contemplating the difference between feelings and emotions, it seems that predominantly, emotions have a conscious or cognitive energy about them whereas feelings have an instinctual energy, are more submerged in the deeper layers of our psyche and are more difficult to access with direct cognitive methods. Nevertheless, the two are difficult to separate. A response to a situation may be a combination of instinct or self preservation, the underlying state of mind, cognition or memory. Murphy, in *A Return to Spirit*[59], writes that feelings are instinctual or conditioned reactions to what humans find pleasant or unpleasant; whereas emotions are more complex responses to reality and flow on from feelings. In theory, emotions rather than feelings are closer to our conscious awareness and therefore should be easier for us to understand. We often find that things are not quite that simple because of the connection between feelings and emotions. Together they are deeply embedded neural, hormonal and chemical brain and body circuits which can prove very difficult to change.

So it appears that there is a continuum of emotions beginning with deep instinctual and unconscious feelings such as are involved with our basic survival as humans. Then we have emotions that are culturally or socially inherited and that come from our group consciousness, which evolved to enhance our group cohesion. We also have emotions on an individual level, which may involve both deeply unconscious and higher level conscious cognitive factors. Thinking analytically is a relatively new phenomenon, developmentally and evolutionarily speaking, although we haven't lost our animal instincts either. There are

59 D Murphy, *A Return to Spirit*, EJ Dwyer, Australia, 1997, p.214.

many different theories to explain emotions. Modern psychology and many spiritual traditions recognise the importance of our underlying mind state when interpreting emotions and acting on them. Both of these disciplines teach awareness of mind when working with emotions.

Because our emotions often influence our decision making, it is important to take some time exploring them. The strength of our emotion may have us believing that the emotion is based on a truth, whereas the emotion may be based on an outdated belief that our ego is holding onto very strongly. Emotions play a crucial role in our interactions with others because they reflect what we perceive to be true, what we think and what we feel and additionally, some emotions have arisen out of societal and cultural factors and so this seems to normalise them. Learning about our emotions, especially the intense ones, is worth investing time and energy in, so that we can better understand the mechanisms that drive us. Unconscious emotional responses can cause much interpersonal conflict.

There are several ways that we can begin to work with developing more awareness of our emotions, particularly the troublesome ones.

- Dream work, as promoted by the Swiss psychiatrist Carl Jung, is an excellent way to explore the depths of our unconscious feelings that give rise to emotions. Our dreams can be quite explicit pointers, showing us exactly what emotions in the present we need to be aware of, and the connection they have with events from our past.
- Psychotherapists, psychologists, counsellors and analysts are all trained to provide a safe space from which to explore emotions, to express them and to learn from them. If we have difficulty with feelings being overwhelming, unbalanced or persistent, or if we have difficulty accessing feelings, there are many professionals

who can guide and assist.
- Journal writing is another way to develop mindfulness of feelings. This can provide a safe avenue for expressing emotions, as well as acknowledging their presence and how they fluctuate and change over time.
- Artistic expression through art therapy has become a well-recognised form of expression for feelings and emotions in cases where children, adolescents and adults are incapable of verbal expression.
- Meditation methods which may help with developing awareness of emotions can include mindfulness meditation and insight meditation. Mindfulness meditation helps us to observe our emotions repeatedly and non judgementally; insight meditation encourages us to sit with an emotion or issue and investigate its nature very deeply.

Full Circle

We often begin meditation training with a supposedly simple practice like mindfulness. However, this skill is a very complex one to learn, especially for us who live where life is fast and our minds are even faster. We think mindfulness practice is too easy, so we move on to other practices. It is often not until we have tried the full gamut of other practices, and have meditated for many years, that we realise we are back where we started from, only at the end learning the importance of mindfulness/awareness.

It many ways, mindfulness or awareness practice is the most important practice of all because it is the basis of all meditations. But not only this, it can be used in every moment of our waking lives as well. Every second, every moment, can be used for mindfulness practice. Every bad day, every sickness when we are too sick to meditate, every deep emotion, every difficult relationship interaction, and every challenge can be used as fuel for mindfulness practice. It is the gold standard of meditation because it pervades every moment of our lives, not just the time we spend in sitting meditation. In a way it is the completion of the circle.

General Advice When Starting to Meditate

- Make meditation a priority or it won't happen.
- Try to practice at the same time and in the same place every day.
- Meditation is a skill that needs constant practice like any other life skill.
- Have faith that meditation will work; be positive about it.
- Use a technique that appeals to you.
- Use the simplest method that works and stick to it for a reasonable time.
- Enlist help from a teacher or group if you struggle with motivation.
- Learn some five minute meditations or spot meditations to do during the day.
- Try to do some sitting meditation every day in a stable posture.
- Create a quiet space, minimising distractions, thus making it easier to learn.
- Start small and build up the time.
- Close eyes to minimise distractions, or half open them if you struggle to stay awake.
- The best time of the day to practice is early morning, although sunset is also a good time.
- Movement meditation is a good adjunct or alternative to sitting meditation.
- Reading a passage of a spiritual text with awareness can be thought of as a daily practice.
- Don't give up – persevere. Developing the skill takes time.
- The intention to grow in awareness is everything.
- Stimulants, alcohol and recreational drugs hinder effective meditation.

- Try being in nature and appreciating its beauty as an alternative to meditation.
- Watch the mind and emotions during the day, non-judgementally. Simply observe.
- Be gentle with yourself, there is no rush.

CHAPTER FIVE
AWARENESS OF DREAM
AND THE SHADOW

In the previous chapter we defined and discussed two aspects of mind called the conceptual mind and the natural mind. Now we explore further the conceptual mind, dividing it into two parts: the conscious mind and the unconscious mind. It is the unconscious mind and its strong link to our emotions, which is the subject of this chapter. If we aim to make our lives more conscious then we will also be interested in bringing our unconscious material into our awareness. Understanding dreams is closely linked to this investigation of our unconscious mind. This is such an important subject because our ability to delve into our own unconscious mind profoundly affects the image we have of ourselves, how we see others, how we present ourselves in the world and how we interact with others.

If I Were to Say to You That There is a Way in Which You Can:

- process the day's events without any effort on your part;
- provide your life with compensation for what it has missed out on during the day;
- see your talents and gifts;
- become clearer in your relationships, particularly intimate ones;
- become more balanced in mind, body and inner energy;
- understand your masculine and feminine psychological makeup;
- see the aspects of yourself that others see but you are unaware of;
- through your emotional complexes and patterns of reacting;
- uncover old memories to help you understand your present self better;
- access wisdom/the Self/universal energy;
- access creativity;
- receive warnings or predictions about your future life direction;
- help you on your way to individuation or personal growth;
- help you to integrate the unconscious aspects of your personality with the conscious aspects;
- receive advice and direction on particular issues;
- develop awareness while in the dream or sleeping state;
- dialogue with the people in your dreams;
- develop compassion for yourself;
- better understand the concerns common to all humanity and look at areas of your life that need attention.

What Would You Think?

Imagine being able to access all this help with our day-to-day lives!

Well, it is available, every night, in our dreams. We may not receive all of these benefits every night, but over time we will observe that our dreams touch most of these areas for our own personal benefit. They are like having our own wise teacher standing by, waiting for us to ask for assistance with life. This teacher knows all about us already and knows where we have been and where we are headed. This teacher also wishes the best for us. Are we ready to take up this challenge?

As outlined in the list above, dreams bring a huge repertoire of uses. For instance, we are told that dreams have the function of restoring our psychological balance. In addition to reflecting and absorbing the events of our daily lives, dreams can also bring up material that we have never consciously thought about before. We may receive inspiration through dreams. It is well-known that some musical people have received whole music scores in dreams. We may also receive material about our lives that we cannot possibly know already, at least with our conscious minds. I remember a time in my own life when I was desperate to know whether or not I would ever meet another life partner. I asked for a dream and that night I dreamt of a man who was quiet, who walked behind me on a walking track and who had an accent. In later years, six years later to be exact, when I met this man I realised that the dream exactly portrayed our first date, which was a walk in the bush, with this man quietly walking behind me. Of course he had an accent as well!

Dreams can advise about spiritual practices, letting you know when it is time to move on, or change to a different practice with a different emphasis. Dreams can access our spiritual guide. Dream is the impartial messenger – the conduit from within. If you need guidance about a particular decision ask your dream for direction. I have found that if I have a problem that is in my mind during the day and I focus on the issue before going to bed and continue to reflect on it as I'm going to sleep, often I will receive a dream relating to that issue. It is as though the waking consciousness needs to be saturated with the issue for it to have a greater chance of percolating towards and connecting with the unconscious.

The main benefit of working with our dreams is to increase our self-awareness. The dream can be thought of as a key with which we can unlock our own inner secrets. They give us continual, specific information about ourselves and our egos. One very important effect of working on our dreams over time, is that they help us to develop self-compassion. People who pursue the path of self-development often become acutely aware of their faults. With dream work we see more clearly, the slow and intricate web of our life and we develop understanding and acceptance of why we are who we are. This self-compassion is an important aspect of dream work because self-compassion makes for a happier life. Additionally, from learning how to be gentle with ourselves, we then progress to developing compassion for others. Compassion for self and others is the initial step towards making our world a happier place.

There are both Eastern and Western ways of working with dreams. One Western method called Jungian dream analysis explores the work of Carl Jung and his idea that dreams communicate messages from the unconscious mind to the conscious mind through their content of images and symbolism which must be interpreted.[60] One Eastern method is Tibetan Buddhism's way of working with the states of dream and sleep. This is a different approach as it aims to bring about greater awareness, not of the content of the dream but of the states of consciousness inherent in dreaming and sleeping.[61] As this book is a mix of Eastern and Western ideas, let's look at both but first of all we need to answer the question...

What are Dreams?

A dream is the spontaneous production of symbols and images which arise during the REM cycle of our sleeping. REM stands for rapid eye movement which occurs with a certain type of

60 C Jung, *Man and his Symbols*, Penguin, Arkarna, 1990.
61 Tenzin Wangyal Rinpoche, *The Tibetan Yogas of Dream and Sleep*, Snow Lion, New York, 1998.

brain wave pattern and other changes during a particular stage of sleep that lasts approximately ninety minutes during a typical nights' sleep.[62] We do not dream during deep sleep or during waking consciousness and it is also known that everyone dreams, although not everyone will remember their dreams. It appears from scientific research that we all need our REM sleep and if we are deprived of this we suffer psychologically – without it we become anxious, irritable and we have trouble concentrating.

We could say that dreams help us to 'digest life' by playing events back to us so that we have the opportunity to absorb life's events and learning. Dreams can also have the function of being a rehearsal for events that are worrying us; they may give the conscious mind an opportunity to reflect on how best to deal with a specific situation in our waking lives. The dream, however, can only be accessed through a small window of opportunity, the conscious remembering of the dream.

Every experience in life has an element of what we are aware of and what we are not aware of. We are aware of that part of the experience that our conceptual minds can understand but we are unaware of what we don't fully grasp and that is what goes into the unconscious. The unconscious simply contains the totality of our experience. This general unconsciousness is the lot of human beings until they reach full enlightenment or they become fully aware.

The waking mind, housed in the neocortex, is concerned with the day-to-day activity of putting plans and values into action. The dreaming mind, thought to originate in the brainstem, the biological seat of our feeling memory, feeds information to the ego or waking mind, reflecting back to us what really is worrying us at a deep level. The brainstem stores our fears and it stores memories from the past, especially of pain and survival. It remembers, like an elephant. It advises on the basis of past

62 Dalai Lama, *Sleeping, Dreaming and Dying*, Wisdom Publications, Boston, 1997, pp.23-52.

history and past experience, perhaps over generations. In our dreaming we seem to be able to access this knowledge and experience of the personal and collective past. In a combination of past history, wisdom and future prediction, the dreaming self definitely offers up a non-judgmental picture of the general direction one is taking in life and what to watch out for and what could be changed.

The dreams that different people have may access this feeling-emotional-memory part of themselves or they may access the wisdom side. A 'wise' dream is recognised as being different from our usual dreams – it will contain images totally unrelated to our everyday life. Bon Buddhist master, Tenzin Wangyal Rinpoche calls these wise dreams, dreams of clarity. He describes three types of dreams – dreams of samsara, dreams of clarity and dreams of clear light.[63] Clear light dreams are rare indeed and they are said to be "...a state free from dream, thought and image..." Dreams of clarity, or wisdom, result from greater awareness in the dream state and are less deluded. It is "...as if something is given to or found by the dreamer..." and these types of dreams are uncommon. In samsaric dreams, which are our usual everyday dreams, our mind reflects on the events of our daily lives.

Our everyday dreams also contain non-expressed information. They can be quite emotional because of the energy source in them which has not been allowed expression in daily life. Dreams are like thoughts, both are forms of energy.

Neuroscience's View of Dreaming

Neurotheologians D'Aquili & Newberg, in *The Mystical Mind*, state that even though there is no direct communication between the unconscious and the conscious mind (they call the conscious ego the primary brain circuit and the unconscious, a secondary

63 Tenzin Wangyal, *The Tibetan Yogas*, pp.61-64.

brain circuit), the former can clearly affect the latter in less direct ways and the unconscious can manifest itself in the form of an emotional response.[64]

Norman Doidge in *The Brain That Changes Itself* states that sleep "...helps us to consolidate learning and memory and effects plastic change."[65] In other words, neuronal connections are being changed while we sleep. Sleep appears to enhance neuroplasticity. He also explains the ability of deep emotions to be brought into our awareness through dreams by saying "With instincts turned up and inhibitions turned down, the dreaming brain can reveal impulses normally blocked from awareness."[66] Doidge is confirming that dreams provide a means by which the unconscious can be brought into consciousness.

D'Aquili and Newberg have confirmed that the original brainstem is the seat of deep fears and emotions, which are brought up to waking consciousness through complicated pathways. Along the way they suggest, myth and archetypes may have developed as a result of activation of certain new brain pathways and structures.[67] Basically, they say myths and archetypes are the brain's way of grouping life into some sort of meaning which can apply to common human behaviour, and that these images coming up tend to be visual and they tend to represent behaviours common to the whole human race.[68] The biological, neurological and physiological explanations for the different ways in which primitive material is brought up to consciousness is too complex for the scope of this book but makes for very interesting reading.

From my perspective, our nightly dreaming may contain some of this archaic material but it also contains very modern material, perhaps relating to our previous day. I suggest that

64 D'Aquili & Newberg, p.65.
65 Doidge, p.240.
66 Doidge, p. 240.
67 D'Aquili & Newberg, p.129.
68 D'Aquili & Newberg, p.86.

our dreams therefore weave the archaic inherited patterns of behaviour and deep emotion, situated in the older part of our brain, into our current complex brain activity, including current (closer to the surface) thinking and emotions. This produces an assortment of mostly visual images which reflect our emotional core through the filters of modern life and brain function. We see therefore a wonderful mix of old and new patterns and if we study dreams we are able to see links, not only to our own suppressed emotional core and our own more complex and newer emotions, but also the emotional core of all humanity.

States of Consciousness

The label 'unconscious' (or asleep) is a blanket term which involves levels or degrees. In my own experience, I have been aware, on occasions, that my consciousness leaves my body when I go to sleep. If I am dozing, not deeply asleep, I have sometimes found myself (my consciousness) hovering over the earth. This takes the form of my body lying face down with arms outstretched, flying over the ground. I can look down at the earth that I am passing over. It seems as though my consciousness has left the earth but it hasn't gone very far away. It is still around my body. Other people have had similar experiences.

Deeper sleep seems to be different as the consciousness leaves the body entirely. Sometimes when I am in bed and not yet awake in the early morning, I experience a huge 'whoosh' feeling and I feel my consciousness return to my body as I awake, zooming through a narrow dark tunnel which becomes ever wider as I rise up towards consciousness. It feels like travelling at lightning speed. I can only assume from this experience that going to sleep is indeed similar to dying, as Buddhists believe. There have been reports of people apparently dying, who experience themselves going through a dark tunnel. [69]

---

69 C Mitchell, *Near Death*, Mandarin, Australia, 1996, p.29.

Imagination is another state which straddles our waking self and our dreaming self. Daydreaming is another one. Creativity and intuition are others. There is also a state which is experienced between waking and falling asleep called the hypnogogic state. In this state one often experiences visions or imagery of great beauty and simplicity which are similar to exceedingly clear and simple dreams. These are all different states of consciousness or awareness.

By increasing our awareness of our dreaming selves we are subtly allowing material to permeate from one level of awareness to another. At night when the ego rests, the information stored in the unconscious is able to break through. Maurice Nicoll in his book *Dream Psychology* explains how material accessed from the deeper levels of the psyche in dream can help us see what it is we are in the process of materialising in daily life... "The process (dreaming) may be compared to the growth of a seed buried in the ground. From the surface of the ground it is impossible to tell what is coming up, save by digging down and examining the earth. If we find a hyacinth bulb we can predict that in the process of time a hyacinth will appear. The bulb is the nascent form of the hyacinth. If we look on the bulb as a symbol, then it is a symbol with a prospective meaning. In the same way the symbols that are encountered in the deep levels of the psyche during sleep are the germinating seeds of the flowers that will appear in the consciousness of waking life." [70]

Carl Jung's Theories and Method of Working with Dreams

Sigmund Freud, an Austrian psychiatrist, began to work with understanding dreams as part of treating his patients in the early twentieth century. He was a mentor to and followed by Carl Jung, a Swiss psychiatrist, who dedicated his life to studying dreams and humankind's basic drive towards wholeness, which he called 'individuation'. Jung called his theory and practice

70 M Nicoll, *Dream Psychology*, Samuel Weiser, Maine, 1987, p.119

of psychology 'analytical psychology'; nowadays we use the term 'Jungian analysis'. When this analysis works mainly with dreams then it is called 'Jungian dream analysis'. Analysis is a special form of psychotherapy which works closely with the unconscious. This is why such work is of great interest to someone wanting to become more aware or more conscious about their life. According to the New York Association for Analytical Psychology – "Jungian analysis is a specialized form of psychotherapy in which the Jungian analyst and patient work together to increase the patient's consciousness in order to move toward psychological balance and wholeness, and to bring relief and meaning to psychological growth. At the heart of Jungian analysis is a realignment of conscious and unconscious aspects of the personality with an ensuing creation of new values and purpose."[71]

It was Carl Jung who postulated that all the people in our dreams are actually the unconscious aspects of our own personality and that our unconscious is an aspect of our psyche which is essentially made up of a lifetime of memories and behaviour patterns (which he called complexes). Many of these we have not registered consciously.[72] Suppression occurs when we are unable or unwilling to understand and integrate these experiences. Storage of memories occurs when the conscious mind perceives that it has no use for them at this time and so it puts them away. Imagery is the vehicle by which information is transported into our conscious mind and is described as the language of the unconscious mind.[73]

Because our dreams are mostly presented in symbolic form through imagery, we may have great difficulty understanding them. It is tempting to take dreams literally but most dreams are not about our external world but our internal world. The dream

71 New York Association for Analytical Psychology, *About Jungian Analysis*; Frequently asked Questions, retrieved 8 September 2011, <http://www.nyaap.org/about-jungian-analysis>
72 Jung, *Man*, p.23.
73 Gawler, *The Mind*, p.74

will bring us a message through its symbolic story. Just as the conceptual mind thinks in words, logical thought, concepts and ideas, the unconscious thinks in symbols, images and stories.[74] If we wish to learn the language of the unconscious we must be prepared to learn it as though it is a foreign language

Carl Jung believed that each dream tells the truth about a person's roots and that the dream comes from what he called The Self. Other philosophers have called this same concept God, universal consciousness, divine wisdom etc. have dismissed this fount of knowledge.

To quote Jung:

> "The hero's main feat is to overcome the monster of darkness: it is the long-hoped-for and expected triumph of consciousness over the unconscious. The coming of consciousness was probably the most tremendous experience of primeval times, for with it a world came into being whose existence no one had suspected before. "And God said, 'Let there be light' 'is the projection of that immemorial experience of the separation of consciousness from the unconscious."[75]

As well as our psyches being made up of multiple traits, Jung found that we are also made up of both male and female aspects which he called the animus and the anima, and that these figures appear in our dreams to show us their state of balance or imbalance in our psyches. The anima or animus character has the opposite gender as us in our dreams (while our shadow aspect has the same gender as us in our dreams). The Chinese call this same concept of male/female, the yin and the yang of our makeup. Jung taught that it is very important for us to uncover and to be aware of both our male and female aspects and bring

74 J Sanford, *Dreams and Healing*, Paulist Press, New York, 1978, p.18.
75 C Jung, 'The Psychology of the Child Archetype', *Collected Works,* vol 9 part 1, Princeton University Press, 1969.

them to awareness and balance. Within us there is a constant struggle to balance opposing forces: light and dark, male and female, positive and negative. The process of individuation is the process of bringing unity between all these opposing forces in ourselves. This unity is the desire that we have for inner peace, wholeness and completion.

Jung's Idea of The Shadow

If we think of a shadow we realise that it is always with us but often hidden from our sight. We also don't notice our shadow unless there is both light and dark and even then we need to make a conscious effort to look for it. We have to put some energy into this process. This is the work of dream analysis, shining light onto our unconscious mind and noticing what has always been there – a part of us.

In our dreams our shadow appears in the form of other people or even animals. The feeling that arises when we think of this dream character or animal in daily life is exactly the trait that we ourselves possess but perhaps are unaware of. For instance, I may have a dream which includes my cousin. When I am awake again and I think about my cousin I bring to mind one word that best describes her at that moment. The word will perfectly describe an aspect of myself that I am not acknowledging and that I need to be more aware of.

According to Robert A Johnson, our shadow is a part of our unconscious which is the dumping ground for all the characteristics of our personality that we disown.[76] He explains that we divide the self into an ego, which is the acceptable side of ourself, and a shadow, which is the part that is not accepted by society and so has been submerged. It is the process of civilisation in our particular culture which determines what is acceptable and what is not. To be accepted by our society, we

---

76 R Johnson, *Owning Your Own Shadow*, Harper Collins, New York, 1993, p.ix.

hide those parts which we know won't be accepted and this becomes our shadow side. Jung maintained that the ego and the shadow balance each other and that one can't exist without the other.

To quote Jung again: "The psychological rule says that when an inner situation is not made conscious, it happens outside as fate. That is to say, when the individual remains undivided and does not become conscious of his inner opposite, the world must perforce act out the conflict and be torn into opposing halves."[77]

How true this is. We notice that life presents us with the very situations that we wish to avoid. If we don't learn these lessons, we find life repeating itself, especially in our relationships. Everything in us which is unconscious, repressed, undeveloped and denied will eventually come out.

Archetypes are collective shadow material – common themes for all of humanity. The anima or the animus are archetypal forces. Archetypes are the common psychic structure of humanity. We as humans have a common physical form which is easy enough to see; in the same way we also have a common mental form. This is the stored memory that each person has of the whole human race. Such memories inform how we respond in particular situations regardless of our culture. An example could be – how we act when we are in love. This behaviour is similar all over the world. These are collective responses ingrained in us over thousands of years and even today we carry these memories in our consciousness. The collective unconscious contains learned memory from the past. Jung believed that certain archetypal forms (for instance snakes, the cross, the circle, the house, a baby) symbolise age old problems which are common to all of humanity and need to be interpreted in the context of life's journey.

---

77 C Jung, 'Christ: A Symbol of the Self', *Collected Works*, vol 9 part 2, AION, Taylor and Francis, 1959.

The shadow side can appear in our lives as irrational and instinctual behaviour over which we appear to have little control. It is one of the main determiners of our emotional behaviour. Jung also taught that the shadow is capable of containing the best aspects of ourselves: we see this process happening in people with poor self-esteem or lacking in confidence who hero worship others, not realising that they are projecting their own qualities onto someone else. People who are undergoing difficulties with life transfer all their hopes onto the teacher or therapist who, it is hoped, will rescue them from their problems. It is inevitable that these same people will eventually begin to see that their heroes are not perfect at all; they too contain the light and the shadow together. Uncovering our shadow material may help us to acknowledge and foster these qualities so that we may 'own' them again.

Everyone has a shadow side. Just as an example: we may be required to work with someone whom we strongly dislike and we may have a very strong, almost irrational, reaction to this person. If we examine why this is we may find that the qualities that we really dislike in this other person will usually be the exact opposite of what we believe about ourselves. If we find ourselves reacting strongly in this way to someone, we can be sure that we are looking at an aspect of our own shadow. What happens is that we project onto other people parts of ourself that we don't acknowledge in ourself. These parts or behaviours that we see in that other person, make us feel very uncomfortable. We can test our reaction by asking others how they feel about this particularly 'annoying' person. We often find that not everyone reacts as strongly as we do. This is because we are projecting our own shadow (in this case a particular fault that we don't own up to) onto them. A similar process operates when we are in a state of romantic love. We project our own good qualities (which we haven't owned in ourselves) onto the desired partner.[78] In the same way, when we long for the company of a very close

78 R Johnson, *The Psychology of Romantic Love*, Arkana, Penguin, London, 1987.

friend or relative, we are projecting our own unacknowledged strengths and good qualities onto that other person. We believe that we can only access these qualities through association with the other person, whereas in reality we all have these same characteristics but they may be undeveloped or repressed.

Another easily recognised example might be that we find our partner, a family member, a friend or a stranger, repeating an unacceptable pattern of behaviour that he/she can't seem to improve despite all the resolutions made and good intentions to change. We then may become quite frustrated with this person and call them weak or lacking in discipline. It is possible that this person is reflecting back to us an aspect of our own shadow. Are we so annoyed at this person because we have similar failings which we are afraid of acknowledging? At a deep level we may fear this same quality in ourself. It is usually a quality that we store away privately and never admit to, even with our closest friends. Relationships are very effective at pointing out to us our shadow side and working with the shadow side is a wonderful way to work on our close relationships. Dream analysis has the effect of helping us to modify our self-constructed self-image – this is in effect a reality check. By simply allowing dreams and their meaning to percolate through into our waking consciousness, they remain in our awareness and over time influence our behaviour. Dreams confront these dark/shadow aspects of ourselves in a non-judgmental way. The very first thing we have to do if we are to begin looking at our shadow side is to be willing to take 100% responsibility for our lives. We are working here, with uncovering the fiction of the ego. Until we can do that we won't have the honesty to deal with our shadow side. We will simply ignore it or deny it.

In our shadow, we hide our weaker qualities such as our greed, our hypocritical behaviour or our domineering qualities and by doing so, they go straight into our unconscious. Unfortunately these qualities have not gone away and they will continue to exert pressure on how we interact with others, from this deeper level. Unless we work on owning our shadow, it will push us into uncomfortable interpersonal situations that we would much rather avoid. These types of interactions often leave us with the distinct feeling that we didn't handle them very well. We feel unsatisfied, somehow, and know that we can do better.

Dream work is often humiliating as our deepest, darkest secrets and fears will emerge. The work is a process of ego cleansing or ego integration which helps us to acknowledge our deep vulnerability as humans. We learn from the great psychoanalyst, Carl Jung, that unless our shadow side is made conscious, we never get a chance to correct it. He says that our shadow side "...consists not just of little weaknesses and foibles, but of a positively demonic dynamism." Jung describes our shadow as having so much repressed energy that he calls it a 'raging monster'. He says that people themselves have no idea of the war raging in their unconscious.

Not being able to accept criticism of ourself is a common shadow problem. If we can't accept outer criticism, it is highly probable that our inner critic is still happily resident in our unconscious shadow. The inner critic, which can be incredibly harsh, has developed alongside our ego. We must learn to recognise it – to be aware of its presence and its power over us. In our Western psyches this part of our shadow has sometimes become a hugely negative pattern of unconscious thinking, perhaps a key factor in the development of anxiety and depression. The ego and inner critic have our main priority in life as being good, successful, accepted or secure, and if we are unaware of this pattern, we will continue to live according to the ego's demands, full of self-deceit, self-criticism and ego inflation.

How to Understand our Dreams, Jungian Style

Remembering our dreams on a regular basis so that we may explore them requires a conscious effort on our part and a willingness to spend time contemplating the context and meaning of each dream. In addition, it is difficult to see the real meaning of a dream because we see the content from the context of our own mental filters. Real understanding involves enlisting the help of a professional and impartial dream analyst and the process of analysis often takes many years.

Jungian dream analysis works at one's own pace. The process is actually very clever. It is a sort of puzzle as the dreams are not literal but symbolic. I have always been intrigued by my dreams and I continue to find them fascinating. I can imagine that it must be similar to a mathematicians delight in working out an equation or mathematical theory. There is something hugely satisfying in working out the meaning of a dream.

Every dream has a message no matter how insignificant or short the dream seems. Every dream is important and the complexity of the dream reflects our own complex psychological natures. We get to see through the dream symbols that we are not simple beings. All the characters in our dreams show us different aspects of our personalities. Possibly this is why we sometimes have such difficulty making decisions about things. We have all these distinct and different personalities within us, which compete for attention. Our total character is made up of all of these people who live within.

Dream work is not a six session type of therapy. The unconscious does not divulge its secrets easily or quickly. This lengthy process also allows time for the conscious mind to integrate what comes up before progressing. If the messages of the dreams become too difficult to assimilate into consciousness, or we decide that we don't want to go any further into them, we will simply cease to remember the dream. Or the dreams may continue on in the same theme until that emotion or difficulty has been acknowledged and accepted, which may mean months of intermittent dreams about the same issue. If we watch the progression of these dreams we gradually see the content and the feeling changing as we work on and change or absorb these same issues in our waking life.

The very fact that we are resistant to the truth about ourself is cleverly incorporated into dreams and we cannot understand the symbols with the same skill as a professional, who sees us impartially and who has spent many years learning the meaning of symbols in dreams. Dream work is a two-way street. The client presents the dream with its life context and associations and the analyst provides the knowledge for decoding it and the impartial observations. There can be no mistaking, however, that the analyst has brought forward a personal opinion, it is the dream which does the 'showing'. We have the experience of an "a-ha" moment when the meaning of the dream suddenly clicks into place – it is like the light being turned on in a dark room. Once the dream analyst and the client have agreed on the probable meaning or message of the dream, the client then goes away and reflects on the message of that dream for a period of time. My dream analyst informs me that just by having and recalling the dream, and reflecting on it during the day, the dream begins to work all by itself in effecting change. The material is slowly becoming conscious.

Anyone can learn to remember their dreams and write them down as soon as they awake. The intention or the will to remember is the important thing. It also helps if we can reflect on that dream during the day, leaving it floating in the background of our mind and retrieving it from time to time during the day. A hectic lifestyle and an ultra busy mind will not help this process to happen unless we can set aside a specific time daily to do this work. When documenting a dream, we look for associations of the content of the dream with one's daily life over the preceding few days, particularly emotions and the undercurrents of feeling – and write these down too. These associations may come immediately the dream is written down or they may come later. It is helpful to re-read the dream several times during the day or to set aside a little time to 'digest' the dream.

The language of the unconscious, is feeling, not analysis. Our dreams are full of feelings and the material, which is quite specific to us personally, will only be unravelled if we are able to go deeply into the feelings which the dream evokes. It is in the feeling of the dream, and our ability to stay with that feeling, that the meaning of the dream will emerge.

Jung found that meditation was another way to access the unconscious. He called this 'active imagination'. He found that stillness of mind during meditation allowed imagery, messages, insights and dialogue to arise. Creative people relate that new and complex ideas often arise or are made clear in this way, or that they have received messages imbued with wisdom. Other authors have explained this process as dialoguing with figures in the dream. Alternatively, we can speak the dream aloud to a trusted friend. Insights will often arise as we do this – it is as though we are putting ourselves back into the feeling of the dream as we do this.

John Sanford also suggests people paint their dreams in colour. He says that the process of doing so often allows insights to arise. Various processes of working with dreams, whether speaking with the dream figures, contemplating the content and feeling of the dream, writing the dream down, speaking the dream aloud, or painting the dream – all allow us to reflect on the dream and by so doing we allow meaning to spontaneously emerge from the dream. Any of these methods provide the link between what is conscious in our minds and what is not conscious. They provide a means to access our emotional history.

A valuable benefit of dream work is that we learn the importance of expressing feelings in our daily life as they arise. We are no longer children, and feelings if expressed early enough rather than suppressed, will be much less intense and damaging. We will learn that they are a natural part of being human. In fact, having awareness of our feelings is one of the qualities that define us as human. If we can allow ourself to be honestly vulnerable with our loved ones, they too will learn the importance of being authentic. We all need to find a way in which our shadow and our conscious personality can live together.

Tibetan Buddhism's Way of Working With The Shadow

Rob Preece's book, *The Psychology of Tantra,* explains that, traditionally, the Hinayana Buddhist practices, through the method of Vipassana meditation, encouraged practitioners to observe the ego patterns in their thinking and everyday situations. However the deep cause of ego patterns can remain hidden despite years of meditation practice. Buddhist Tantric work on the other hand, is said to work with the shadow side through the use of symbols and ritual, which are universal rites of transformation.[79] Tantra is said to acknowledge the presence of a dark side and uses the awareness of these forces to help us coexist with them.

The ritual, symbolism and mystery of Tibetan Buddhism are said to resonate deeply in the unconscious mind and the Tantric deity can embody the shadow in a similar way that Carl Jung's archetypes do. The Tantric way of working with archetypal forces is complex to say the least and requires a considerable amount of time and practice. We would require first many years of laying the foundations of Buddhist practice before attempting work with Tantric deities. It is useful, none the less, to understand that Tibetan Buddhist Tantra has its own acknowledgement of the dark side of our natures and has developed practices to work with these issues.

79 Preece, pp.179-182.

Tibetan Buddhism's Way of Approaching Dreams and Sleep

Dreams and Yogic/Subtle Energy

Buddhism considers the origin of dreaming to be an interface between our physical body and our subtle energy body and the 14th Dalai Lama states that Tibetans have been involved in dream work since the time of Naropa in the 11th century.[80] These practices were only done by the experienced few, however, and were not taught to the general public or to beginning meditators. The work with dream and sleep were called yogic practices because they involved the meditator learning how to control subtle energy in the body in order to influence the consciousness during dream, deep sleep and the death process.

The traditional Tibetan Buddhists teach that the practice of developing awareness in the dream and sleeping states begins with learning to move one's subtle energy into one's central channel through meditation or yogic practices.[81] The specialised practices included in *the Six Yogas of Naropa*, include the practices of inner heat – which relates to the movement of subtle energy; the illusory body practice – which relates to our view of reality and awareness; clear light practice – which is an experience associated with both death and dreaming; consciousness transference and forceful projection – which are practices developed to assist in the dying process; and the bardo yoga practices – which are said to help one after death. The explanation of dream yoga is usually found in the illusory body section and that of sleep yoga is usually found in the clear light section. These practices are advanced yogic practices and although well-documented in texts written in languages other than Tibetan in the last thirty years, they tend not to be practiced except by dedicated practitioners of Tantric practices. These are not beginner's practices, however reading and learning about

80 Dalai Lama, *Sleeping, Dreaming and Dying* p.38.
81 GH Mullin, *The Six Yogas of Naropa*, Snow Lion Publications, New York, 2005, p.61.

them can give us a whole new perspective on the mysteries of sleep, dreaming and death. We see how very advanced were the practices of yogic meditators in the old Tibet.

Is All of Life a Dream?

In Buddhist texts we often hear that life here is all a dream and we are the dreamers dreaming the dream. This statement is difficult to understand from a Western perspective. To explain: our minds create our waking reality i.e. our reality is made up of our individual interpretation of events – in the same way, our minds create the reality of the dream while we are asleep. It is the same process going on whether we are awake or asleep. Tibetan Buddhists teach that just as one can learn to transform life by transforming one's mental processes, i.e. thoughts and attitudes, so one can learn to transform the dream by recognising that one is dreaming, that it is only a dream, and by changing our mental processes in the dream. It is the aim of Tibetan Buddhism to control the mind which is dreaming the dream. It says that transforming both daily life and dream life require awareness or the quality of wakefulness with regard to our mental processes and that this can be learned whether we are awake, dreaming or asleep.

The Stages of Sleep

The Dalai Lama in *Sleeping, Dreaming and Dying* states that there are four well-known stages in falling asleep.[82] These stages correlate well with modern sleep research studies, which is surprising as the Buddhist meditators arrived at the same conclusions as scientists but without technology. They simply noticed experientially how the mind moves through different stages during sleep. They were able to do this because they had trained their minds to remain aware during sleep.

82 Dalai Lama, *Sleeping, Dreaming and Dying* p.40.

Modern psychological teachers such as Carl Jung and Sigmund Freud brought the remembering of dreams into our Western consciousness but it is quite rare for Western psychologies to teach how to be aware that one is dreaming whilst dreaming and how to be aware in the state of deep sleep that one is asleep. Tibetan Buddhist meditators maintain that if one can develop awareness during the twenty four hours of the day and night, firstly it creates further time and opportunity to integrate and practice the teachings, and secondly it prepares us for our death, which in effect is a long sleep.

Buddhism's View of Dream Content

Tibetan Buddhists who work with dream practices say that modern psychological dream work which analyses dream content is useful for the beginner but for the advanced practitioner, awareness of dream and sleep states is ultimately more valuable than the content.[83] To explain this: Buddhism says that the common dreams that we have come from our desires and wishes – our karmic traces. Tenzin Wangyal Rinpoche says that '...the dream is...a narrative constructed from conditioned tendencies and habitual identities' and that dream practice '... gives us a method of burning the seeds of future karma during the dream.' He says that if we learn to stay aware in the dream the karmic traces will '...self-liberate as they arise and they will not continue on to manifest in our life as negative states.'[84] It is said that karmic traces can be collective as well as individual.

Clear Light Practice, Deep Sleep and Death

The practice of developing awareness in sleep (as opposed to dream) or during the clear light practice goes one step further and is connected with experiencing the Dharmakaya state which

---

83 Tenzin Wangyal, *The Tibetan Yogas*, p.205.
84 Tenzin Wangyal, *The Tibetan Yogas*, p.33.

is said to be the ground or basis of all being.[85] These states are different levels of consciousness according to Buddhism. Buddhists state that by learning how to be aware of sleeping while we are asleep (no mean feat!) we are learning how to remain aware during the death process. Buddhist practices which make use of the sleeping hours to continue with daily awareness practice are specialised, to say the least and they require a fair degree of proficiency in other meditative techniques prior to embarking on them.

It is interesting to read that, according to the Dalai Lama, the experiences of falling asleep and dying are the same – that of the dissolution of the elements which make up a person – and this dissolution is accompanied by differences in the levels of subtle consciousness and differences in the vital/energetic levels.[86] Apparently the clear light of sleep (the deepest level of sleep during the four stages of sleep) is not as deep as the clear light of death but practitioners use it as training for death. In Tibetan Buddhism it is considered very beneficial if one can remain aware during the process of dying and dissolution so as to be able to navigate our way through the mental experiences which arise during our transition from life to death and beyond. If we can do this, we are better able to determine and choose our next birth or ultimately choose the end of the cycle of birth and death. In the Tibetan tradition therefore, dream work seems to be of great importance in preparation for death.

A Book for Westerners

More recently Tenzin Wangyal Rinpoche, a Tibetan Bon Buddhist master, has written a book for Westerners on these complicated practices – *The Tibetan Yogas of Dream and Sleep*.[87] In this book

---

85 See Chogyal Namkhai Norbu, *Dream Yoga and the Practice of Natural Light*, Snow Lion, New York, 2002.
86 Dalai Lama, *Sleeping, Dreaming and Dying*, p.162.
87 Tenzin Wangyal, *The Tibetan Yogas*.

Tenzin Wangyal Rinpoche advises us to look to our experience in dreams to see how we will fare in death. If we are unaware in the dream state then we will be unaware during the process of dying and death. He says that the only way we will achieve this awareness in the dream and death state is to make all of our life practice, no matter what we are doing. Conversely, through working to be more aware in the dream state we can cultivate greater awareness in every moment of our waking life. He emphasises that the most important thing is cultivating awareness at all times, day and night. Once we learn daytime awareness we can then respond to dream events in positive and creative ways. Rinpoche teaches that dream yoga applies to all experience, to the dreams of the day as well as the dreams of the night.

Final Thoughts

Working with the content and symbols of our unconscious mind seems a natural progression when we begin to realise that years of spiritual work still leave us with unchanged, unconscious behaviour patterns. Before we can begin to learn the Eastern spiritual method of awareness of dreaming and sleeping, or to have experiences of dream yoga and the practices of natural light, we have to deal with the ego. There is no point in attempting advanced spiritual practices without having done the preparation or ground work first.

When we work with dream content, as per Western psychological methods, we soon discover that dream content reflects back deep emotional issues from our past. The practices of the dream and sleep Yogas discussed above do not aim to solve life issues but rather to skip this whole step of emotional issues and simply go straight to the experience of integrating all moments – waking, sleeping, dreaming and dying – with the clear light. When this is done, liberation is said to be the result.[88]

88 Tenzin, p.169.

Sometimes, when I have been in deep meditation I have experienced old emotional pain returning, in graphic detail. This does not happen often but when it does, I re-experience in vivid detail and unbearable pain, images of one or other of my children suffering. This is the ultimate pain for any mother and I am usually very distressed by these occurrences. The trauma seems very real as though it is happening in the present moment. My Jungian analyst would say that I am replaying deep emotional wounding from my own childhood. We all experience some degree of this. The fact that this emotional pain is experienced so intensely is due to the fact that during meditation we are in a state of consciousness which is lighter than a dream. We are much more alert. It therefore seems very real.

On the other hand, I have had dreams in which I experience similar emotional pain i.e. one or the other of my children is hurt or suffering, but the suffering is less intense because the dream state is a lower state of consciousness. When I bring these dreams of suffering to my dream analyst and we work through them, I find that the deep underlying issue is discussed, acknowledged and processed. The dream relives some memory from the depths of my childhood in a story and image form, so that the conscious mind can grasp what is going on, in and around the memory. The dream explores this memory safely, in a form that can be tolerated. It is painful, but not excruciatingly so. It seems to provide a bridge between the past and the present in a way that this deep memory can be worked with. It provides a context for working with the emotional trauma which meditation does not seem to do, for me at least. Is it that my Western psyche responds best to Western techniques in dealing with traumatic emotional pain? I'm not absolutely sure, but it would seem so.

For those of us working in both Western and Eastern disciplines, it can be difficult to obtain advice because our meditation master doesn't understand modern therapies in depth and our Western psychological practitioner doesn't understand Tibetan or Bon Buddhist practices in depth. I have found it imperative to trust my own judgement, after carefully reflecting on what is helpful for me and what is not, and to trust my own inner wisdom. I also try to keep an open mind about things that I don't fully understand or which I am not proficient at and I am hoping as time goes on that I will continue to be guided intuitively to a blending of philosophies that is appropriate to my particular personality and life history. This is all we can do – work with what presents itself to us to the best of our ability and trust that our inner work will, step by step, lead us in the direction in which we need to go.

CHAPTER SIX
AWARENESS OF SUBTLE ENERGY

Subtle energy is the Buddhist (and increasingly Western) term used to describe what is also called 'prana' in India or 'chi' in China. Islam and Sufism also acknowledge the existence of this force within and around the body and Christians call it 'spirit'. This energy has also been called 'the universal life force'. The Chinese have an additional term, 'jing', to denote the essence of the life force itself. In Tibet, subtle energy is called lung meaning 'energy-wind' and refers to the body's internal energy. This energy is said to traverse the internal channels, 'nadis', and which congregate at the energy centres or chakras which run alongside the spine. In Tibetan Buddhism, lung or subtle energy is closely associated with mind and consciousness. It is difficult to explain this energy in Western terms except to say that Western science is increasingly coming to understand that there is an energetic link between body and mind[89] and that there exists a human energy field which is "...a frequency domain beyond our normal field of perception..."[90]

89 M Talbot, *The Holographic Universe,* Grafton Books, London, 1991, p.86.

In modern times there have been suggestions from scientists that subtle energy is equivalent to the autonomic nervous system, which is composed of both the sympathetic and the parasympathetic branches and which is essentially a bodily system of nervous system innervation and inhibition. However, in the main spiritual traditions of the world it is known as a subtle, energetic dimension of the body which transcends time and space and which pervades the entire universe.[91] Furthermore, it is said in many traditions that all life depends on this vital energy.[92] It is considered a life force. When we take a look at modern particle physics shortly, we will begin to see the parallels between this ancient knowledge and modern science.

Unique to the Tibetan and the Hindu spiritual traditions, an array of yogic practices has been developed which aim to control or move this subtle energy throughout the body. In the Tibetan tradition it is maintained that subtle energy is intimately linked with the mind, with the emphasis on subtle energy affecting mind states.[93] The Tantric practices of Tibet are largely concerned with working with the inner subtle energy to purify and transform the mind, while the practices called the Inner Yogas are said to have the effect of loosening karmic blockages in this subtle energy system.[94] The meditational practices of Tibetan Vajrayana work with this subtle energy as do practices such as qigong, tai chi and yoga.

Here is a definition of subtle energy from the book *Sleeping, Dreaming and Dying* by the Dalai Lama[95] from the Tibetan Buddhist point of view: "Subtle energy-mind is the most subtle constituent of the subtle body. It refers to both the subtle vital energy and the subtle mind. It also refers to the clear light, and it is the aspect of the mind-body continuum which travels

90 Talbot, pp.165-168.
91 R Ray, *Secret of the Vajra World – the Tantric Buddhism of Tibet*, Shambhala, Boston, 2002, p.232.
92 Dalai Lama, *The Universe*, p.93.
93 Dalai Lama, p.110.
94 Ray, p.231.
95 Dalai Lama, *Sleeping, Dreaming and Dying*, p.240.

uninterrupted from one life to the next. Some say that it abides as a small sphere in the heart-center."

But what exactly is this subtle energy?

Over my initial years of study and practice I read a lot about the Eastern idea of energy within the body. The Chinese Traditional Medicine system which is very ancient goes into great detail as to the location and effect of these energy pathways on the physical body, however I always found this difficult to understand. A part of my spiritual path has been involved in trying to digest the concept of internal energy and how it affects our ability to live in practical terms. In Western terms, energy in the human body is largely a physical affair. It is a complex idea involving the capacity of our body cells and systems to produce or have inherent in them, genetic, chemical, hormonal, magnetic and electrical energy. We also know from experience that there is a mental aspect to physical energy as well. For instance, my body may be in reasonable condition and I may be getting enough sleep but I may still feel tired. Perhaps I am having difficulties at work or at home that are causing me to feel mentally exhausted – so we see that the energy of the body and the energy of the mind are linked. When we observe everything that we do, think or experience, we see that everything has an energetic basis.

The Dalai Lama in his book *Sleeping, Dreaming and Dying* says that there are three levels of prana (energy) – gross, subtle and very subtle and that the self is made up of gross physical aspects, mental aspects and also of very subtle vital energy. When asked the question of what connects the body, the mind and the very subtle mind, he replies that subtle energy is the base energy which constitutes the elements which then go on to produce matter. Modern physicists, Goldberg and Blomquist in *A User's Guide to the Universe*, support this theory when they state that

"Matter and energy are equivalent..."[96] They explain that "...the electromagnetic field creates an interaction that moves charged particles" and that the Higgs field "creates an interaction that gives a particle mass."[97] Buddhism has identified an all pervasive subtle energy. Now particle physics is identifying several energy fields and the affect they have on particles, and in fact, everything in the universe.

The Dalai Lama also suggests that the very subtle energy is actually the vehicle for karma as it manifests through the inner and outer elements. In Buddhism, the elements are said to be the basis of matter. He says that karma uses energy to travel or manifest, as it were, and it is able to do this because of a two-way interface between the mind and the physical elements. So we see that Buddhism adds the mind into the interaction between energy and mass. Kalu Rinpoche, a Tibetan Buddhist meditation master, backs up what the Dalai Lama says by stating that subtle energy has a reciprocal action with the mind. "...Our body is intimately related to the nadis, prana, and bindus that make up the material support of mind. By acting on the support of mind, one acts on mind itself. There exists indeed a reciprocal action of the mind with this subtle energy system."[98]

Interestingly, modern physicists now know that "...our observations of a system can fundamentally change it..."[99] It appears that the observer in an experiment can change reality in a profound way. Could this be linked to the quality of awareness changing our reality or how we see the world?

If we are to understand what subtle energy is then we need to learn a little physics. Trinh Xuan Thuan an astrophysicist, in *The Quantum and the Lotus* talks about the basis of the universe

---

96 D Goldberg & J Blomquist, *A User's Guide to the Universe*, John Wiley and Sons, New Jersey, 2010, p.191.
97 Goldberg & Blomquist, p.115.
98 Kalu Rinpoche, *Secret Buddhism*, Clear Point Press, California, 2002, p.95.
99 Goldberg & Blomquist, p.47.

in energetic terms.[100] He explains the modern scientific string theory which states that tiny particles of matter aren't the most fundamental elements of the universe, as was previously thought. Traditional Newtonian physics is based on the principle that matter eventually can be broken down into increasingly smaller components until one arrives at the smallest possible particle. Quantum physics has challenged this theory. Quantum actually means very small so quantum physics is the study of very small particles. The current string theory states that particles of matter are actually just vibrations of infinitely small strings of energy and that the greater the amount of energy in the vibration, the greater the mass of the object.[101]

Goldberg and Blomquist continue on to say that '...the more vigorously a string is vibrating, the more massive it is...' and additionally, that modern string theory "...describes the universe as having ten dimensions, plus one for time."[102] Particle physics is going through some very exciting times. Research is suggesting that this quantum energy therefore is the basis of the universe, not tiny particles of matter as we had previously supposed.

Trinh Xuan Thuan in *The Quantum and the Lotus* talks about the origin of our universe as energy in space. "Physicists say that the universe was born from a vacuum – they call it the quantum vacuum – but this vacuum was not calm and peaceful, as you might imagine. The quantum vacuum was seething with energy, even though it contained no matter. What seems to be empty space is filled with energy fields that can be described as waves. In fact the space that surrounds us is filled with a veritable kaleidoscope of waves of different kinds."[103] Goldberg and Blomquist describe this quantum vacuum as a field which is everywhere in the universe

100 M Ricard & Trinh Xuan Thuan. *The Quantum and the Lotus*, Three Rivers Press, New York, 2001, pp.106-109.
101 See also Goldberg & Blomquist, p. 122.
102 Goldberg & Blomquist, p.275.

103 Ricard & Thuan, p.25.

and which is pervaded by a vacuum energy. This energy arises because "...photons keep popping into and out of existence."[104]

In Desmond Murphy's book *A Return to Spirit*, the author writes in the section on quantum physics that all living beings are made up of waves and particles at the subatomic level and that waves and particles are inseparable as the basic stuff of life.[105] Waves and particles exist together as one unit and they affect each other. Matter is waves and particles together and both are constantly changing and emerging into new ways of being. This theory of quantum physics helps to explain how sound vibration (waves of matter) can affect the way our energy is organised in our bodies and our minds. Without any knowledge of quantum physics, one can simply feel this happening. When we sing for instance, we are able to very quickly feel a change in mood or emotion, depending on the music. Music is said to 'lift the spirits'; a very clear layman's phrase showing the link between sound and energy. Similarly, using mantra or chanting seed syllables has a direct effect on one's internal energy and this causes a corresponding change in mind and body. According to Tibetan Buddhism, mantra is said to address the underlying energy-winds.[106]

Let's now look at the Chinese philosophy for the origin of subtle energy. In TCM, chi or energy flows from the atmosphere or environment into our bodies. TCM texts outlining the use of acupuncture are thought to have been written around 2,500 years before Christ. It is believed that the subtle energy channels, if blocked, can lead to congestion and therefore illness on many levels. In the Chinese system of acupuncture, tiny needles are inserted into the surface of the body at certain points which supposedly have the effect of unblocking channels where subtle energy flows and so preventing or treating disease in the body.

From a layperson's point of view, we relate to the word 'energy' with thoughts about physical stamina and endurance.

104 Goldberg & Blomquist, p.191.
105 Murphy, p.122.
106 Preece, p.98.

Not only do our bodily processes involve the use of energy but so do our mental processes. Our Western culture encourages a more-is-better approach to physical energy. The more energy we have, the more we should be able to achieve. When we feel energetic we tend to take on lots of activities until we feel our energy draining away and then we are forced to stop being so energetic for a while. Sleep restores us and we awaken with renewed energy. When we live life moderately without extremes of behaviour and action, it is said that we will have a more reliable stream of energy to utilise. When we are excited or angry or in the grip of other strong emotions, our energy is quickly depleted. Strong emotions can exhaust us. When we die we have essentially run out of energy – our body cells stop producing energy through their chemical processes and there is no more store supply to draw on. According to Buddhism and quantum physics however, there is no permanent loss of energy with death in that all the particles of subatomic energy of which we are made, simply change and are recycled into the universe in a different arrangement. While Buddhism talks about reincarnation; the world of quantum physics talks about the transformation of particles.

Buddhist teachers such as The Dalai Lama and Kalu Rinpoche go one step further and say that it is impossible to separate consciousness and subtle energy. Apparently these are two aspects of an inseparable reality. Rob Preece in *The Psychology of Buddhist Tantra* states that "...every experience of consciousness has a corresponding associated energy-wind."[107] It is beginning to sound as though all experience is basically energy-based, whether we talk about matter, mind, consciousness or subtle energies. They are all interdependent and linked, being all part of the whole of reality.

In the Eastern spiritual traditions it is said that the subtle energy system of the body contains the blueprints of the physical

107 Preece, p.91.

body – in other words, the subtle energy system has a direct link with the health of the physical body. Quantum physicist Amit Goswami in *The Visionary Window* writes, "Western medicine states that life is chemistry...Eastern medicine is aware that the vital body carries the originals (the morphogenetic fields) of which the physical body's organs are representations. The Eastern view acknowledges disease as faulty chemistry in the physical representations of the vital body but recognizes that the fault could stem from the originals in the vital (energetic) body."[108] This is quite a challenging statement from the point of view of Western medicine. Time and further research will tell whether Eastern theories will eventually merge with modern scientific explanations.

Gregg Braden, a scientist and engineer turned quantum physicist, in his book *The Divine Matrix*[109] explains that there is a subtle energy form which underlies the fabric of creation and which appears to work differently from a typical electrical field, as it appears to be a tightly woven web of energy. He states that this divine matrix is the common denominator between the inner and outer worlds or the world of matter and the world of metaphysics (non-matter) and its field seems to be everywhere all the time. He goes on further to say that this field has 'intelligence' and it responds to the power of human emotion. This is the concept of 'God' and 'universal consciousness'. It has been identified and named by other traditions, scientists and religious teachers – the holographic universe[110], universal mind, universal life force,[111] Tao and Spirit. Defining subtle energy now becomes increasingly difficult as it may have no beginning and no end. These are difficult concepts for our mind to grasp.

108 A Goswami, *The Visionary Window, A Quantum Physicist's Guide to Enlightenment*, Shambhala, Boston, 1994, p.227.
109 See G Braden, *The Divine Matrix*, Hay House, USA, 2007.
110 See R Guiley, *Encyclopaedia of Mystical and Paranormal Experience*, Grange Books, London, 1993.

111 See W Tiller,'What are Subtle Energies?' *Journal of Scientific Exploration*, vol. 7, No. 3, 1993.

What we see emerging now are scientists who are showing the modern scientific world that there is indeed an energetic link between body and mind. William Tiller, a scientist from Stanford University in California is such a scientist. In an article written on subtle energy, Tiller states that subtle energy exists in a vacuum state, with magnetic vector potential being the bridge between subtle and physical energies. His article makes fascinating reading. He also regards subtle energy as incorporating spiritual, mental and emotional aspects. He maintains that these subtle energies affect electrical and magnetic fields in the body which in turn affect body chemistry which ultimately affects body structure and body functioning. It seems that this vacuum state of being has much in common with the Tibetan Buddhist concept of universal/wisdom mind[112] and Greg Braden's divine matrix.

'Kundalini' is an Indian expression for a sudden upsurge of subtle energy awakening in a human. This strong energy is said to have the ability to bring about changes in the person and to initiate extra sensitive abilities to heal self and others. Kundalini releases the latent power of heightened consciousness so that new connections can be made between the energetic body and the physical body.[113] We can think of kundalini as an eruption of subtle energy. Needless to say this is not a common occurrence.

In conclusion, it appears from all the above, that matter is actually energy converted into a form which can be seen. Matter is physical and we call it 'real', as opposed to subtle energy which is invisible and can only be sensed by some people and which most of the population regard as 'unreal.' According to the literature from several of the world's oldest religions, subtle energy is the connecting system which connects the physical to the non-physical and as such, it is the medium that underpins mind-body healing. It connects the physical, emotional, mental and spiritual levels of a person. Subtle energy is a type of life

112 Jamgon Kongtrul the Third. *Cloudless Sky,* Shambhala, Boston, 1992, p.24.
113 See G Kieffer, *Kundalini, Empowering Human Evolution: Selected Writings of Gopi Krishna*, Triad Publications, Queensland, 1998.

force, an essence, which innervates the physical body as well as existing outside the body and in the universe.

Becoming Aware of Subtle Energy – My Story

One of my first experiences of feeling subtle energy flow was after I had learnt the practice of Indian Head Massage. This type of bodywork was originally taught by Narendra Mehta, a blind Indian man who practiced as an osteopath as well as practicing other bodywork methods in London and who brought the ancient Indian practice of head massage to London in 1981.[114] Mehta taught a variation of the practice whereby he incorporated 'subtle energy massage' on various points of the head, face, neck and shoulders. He incorporated an Ayurvedic element into the traditional scalp massage that had been practiced in India for thousands of years and called this *Indian Champissage*. He stated that this technique particularly worked on the upper three chakras; chakras being subtle energy centres closely aligned with the spine.

As I practiced this art and learnt to relax myself as well as the client, I began to feel a very subtle tingling in my fingers when placing light pressure on the pressure points of the face and head. At this stage my experience (being the therapist) was very similar to being in a meditation – mentally very still; and my client often reported similar experiences. Often I could feel the energy in my fingertips, flowing through these energy or acupressure points and I learnt to relax and allow the energy to flow without any conscious activity on my part other than performing the head massage according to my usual routine. It amazed me to hear people's reactions as to what had transpired during the head massage. People reported being put into a very deep state of relaxation where time seemed to stand still. Of course not everyone responded in this way but I received this feedback often enough to realise that the technique of

114 See N Mehta, *Indian Head Massage*, Thorson, Harper Collins, London, 1999.

Champissage was enabling some sort of energy to flow more freely within the person and in a health giving way. This was my first direct experience of feeling an unexplained energy whilst working with another person and was the beginning of an exploration of subtle energy in general.

My experiences with subtle energy in meditation had arisen prior to this but I had no teacher at the time to explain this phenomenon to me. About five years later, as I began on the Tibetan Buddhist meditation path and began working with a Western teacher who had been taught according to the Kagyu Tibetan Buddhist lineage, I began to experience not just the subtle energy within but also an energetic connection between myself and a well known meditation master who had died.

Sometimes during meditation and sometimes, at other times during the day or night, I began to experience a non-physical connection with one of my teacher's teachers. Kalu Rinpoche was a Tibetan born meditation master who had begun teaching in the West in 1971. He died in 1989 and I had never met him. The only connection I had with him was through my teacher, who had received teachings from him. For some inexplicable reason, when I opened his book Gently Whispered[115] which contained his teachings and his photo, I felt intense pressure on the crown of my head and a warmth inside as though the book and I belonged together.

As time went on and my meditation practice deepened, I was amazed to notice that in times of great stress or suffering, Kalu Rinpoche would speak to me through my mind, advise me, walk beside me as a friend does, and bathe me in love so that my mental state and energy would completely change. I found this energetic connection amazingly supportive, as though there was a great love emanating from this man who had passed over into death. This happened several times over those years and when I told my teacher about this she explained that there is an

115 See Kalu Rinpoche, *Gently Whispered.*

energetic connection through the lineage in Tibetan Buddhism so that modern practitioners are able to ask for assistance from those who have passed over and who remain available to help us in times of trouble. In Western terms we speak of invisible angels and how they remain around a person to help them. This is a similar phenomenon to the Buddhist level of beings who have passed over. In Buddhism they are called 'Bodhisattvas' – beings who remain available after death to help those who are still on this earth.[116]

We sometimes hear of relatives who have passed over, making contact with their loved ones on earth; speaking to them after their death.[117] These people (souls) are believed to exist in a formless realm after their death and for some time remain able to communicate with loved ones on earth. We know that these things can happen to some people. It appears however that this communication only happens within a set time frame - usually around the death period whereas the communication with angels and bodhisattvas continues on for a very long time.

The following is a personal story which I have not yet been able to explain satisfactorily but which appears to reveal another type of energetic connection between humans and non-human beings. This is another story of beings on a different plane (or perhaps a different dimension) to our material worldly plane, being able to influence and in this case heal through the energy of love.

One day during the 1990s when I was staying in the city for a few days and was out shopping, I suddenly experienced very intense abdominal pain. I managed to get home to the flat that I was staying in. I was alone there. By the time I arrived, the abdominal pain was so intense that I had to lie down on the bed immediately. Because of the intensity of the pain I was incapable

---

116 Kalu Rinpoche, *Gently Whispered,* p.46.
117 Guiley, p.25.

of doing anything to help myself except lie down on the bed. At the time I remember looking at the telephone and thinking 'I hope no one phones because I simply can't get up to answer it.' I didn't move for fear of making the pain worse. I had no pain killers and no one to help me. I went into survival mode.

Suddenly I was aware of my body being transported up high into the atmosphere. My body was horizontal and that was the position in which I was being lifted. I felt exquisitely tender and loving hands, many of them, lifting me gently upwards. I was totally relaxed. As I lay there, I felt hands on me but I didn't feel any pain. I didn't see any bodies or faces and was aware of only my own body and the hands in my abdomen. After a while I felt myself being lowered ever so gently back down again. I thought to myself, 'This is the most love I have ever received in my whole life. This is pure, highest love.' I felt exquisite gratitude and in awe of what had just happened. I felt cherished and adored beyond anything I had ever experienced before.

Next thing I knew, I was back in my little single bed in the flat and my abdominal pain had gone. I looked over at the telephone and at that very moment it rang. I felt as though no time had elapsed since my thought of 'I hope it doesn't ring.' What had happened was not related to our concept of time. Somehow I knew that I had been in a different reality and I was certain that I hadn't been asleep.

I think that perhaps I had been in the unseen or formless world, the world in between. I don't doubt what I experienced for one minute but I don't have a Western scientific explanation for it either. In my experience, the living and the non-living worlds interact sometimes in a way in which energy is exchanged. in my experience the energy was a loving energy. Our modern mind still feels mystified about how this energy flows. Perhaps quantum physics will be able to make sense of it one day.

Spontaneous Healing Through Energy Transfer

My recounting of personal experiences with the healing ability of subtle may help others to understand more about the workings of subtle energy. There is no thought that I, personally, have healed others and there has been no conscious control on my part in the physical healing of certain persons. Nevertheless there is no doubt in my mind that subtle inner energy can flow from one person to another when required and under circumstances where the person allowing the healing energy to flow through them is not doing so under the influence of the ego or for monetary gain.

According to ancient Buddhist texts, the ability to heal is one of the powers or 'siddhis' of the yogins and yoginis - meditators who spent many years in solitary retreat - and who developed these abilities as by-products of their meditation practice.[118] It was understood that talking about these powers only caused problems for the person doing the healing. My feeling is that these occurrences can happen often and spontaneously (especially in our hospitals) but that they are not understood, acknowledged or talked about. This is a sensible approach if the whole episode leads one to feel inflated or to feel a better person than the next person; however in my case I realise this not to be true. At the time of these healings I was in the midst of coping with emotional issues and I felt very insignificant and troubled. I found that I could relate to the suffering of others so easily, as I was suffering myself. Perhaps that is when the healing energy flows best; when there is no ego to get in the way; when one interacts with another in the spirit of mutual suffering and in the hope of alleviating suffering for us all. My heart had been broken open by an unequal and damaging love affair. Being quite a sensitive (and naive at the time) person, I went through immense psychological trauma over this and it took me years and years to recover. Such fragility, emotional pain and vulnerability

118 Dilgo Khyentse, p.222.

can open us up to really experiencing the heart qualities and can awaken us to greater sensitivity generally.

So in that spirit I will recount my personal experience – some events that happened to me and my patients, while I was working as a registered nurse with acutely ill patients in a hospital during the mid-nineties. In my opinion, the stories which follow show that there can be a connection between the subtle inner energy of one person and the subtle energy, and consequently the physical wellbeing of another.

Nursing a Farmer

One day I was nursing a seventy year old farmer who had just experienced a heart attack. He was a lovely man and had never been in hospital before. A day after his heart attack, while he was still resting in bed, his chest pain returned. The pain was so severe that this man required a very large amount of intravenous morphine, but still his pain did not go away. I had called for the doctor who was on his way and still the poor man was in agony; bent over, sweating and clutching his chest, unable to speak. I was unable to do anything else medically for him until the doctor arrived. Without thinking, I sat on the bed beside him, put my arms around him and held him, wishing with all my heart that he didn't have to suffer in this way. Then the doctor arrived, further drug treatment was begun and I stayed to help. After a while the pain was relieved and the doctor diagnosed a further extension of his heart attack. The man survived and a few days later was moved out of the acute area and into a ward bed after thanking me profusely for looking after him. This was not unusual in such an environment where people were often on the brink of death.

Some days later the nurse who was looking after him on the ward came to me for a confidential word. She recounted to me something that the man had told her. He said when he was suffering the dreadful chest pain in the coronary care unit and we were waiting for the doctor, he felt himself being forced into a dark narrow tunnel with light at the end. He said that he didn't want to go into the tunnel and that he was struggling, being pushed along against his will. Then, he said, he felt me sit down next to him and put my arms around him and hold him, and from that very moment he felt the blood begin to stir and circulate around his heart and through his body again. He felt himself come back to being in this world and he emerged from the dark tunnel.

This nurse suggested that I speak with the man, which I did. We hugged and he explained that it had taken him a while to be brave enough to discuss the matter. Once again he thanked me. Soon after that he went home and three months later I heard that he had suffered a final and terminal heart attack, however I also heard that he had been grateful for those final three months to put his affairs in order and to say his goodbyes. This first healing experience affected me very deeply, in fact I was quite shocked for a time, but it awakened me to the possibility of these things happening and so I was more aware the next time it came about.

Nursing Phillip

I was nursing in the same acute area of the hospital when a man came in who had collapsed at home. He was under careful observation and was attached to a cardiac monitor and other medical apparatus. Under my care that morning he had had brief episodes of flat-lining (heart stopping) which were recorded on the monitor, but they were so brief that I questioned the reliability of the outdated technology that we had in use. I called a senior nurse to come and check the man over. We didn't have doctors around in those days – they had to be called in from their medical practices in town. As the senior nurse and I were looking at the man's heart tracing, his heart trace flat lined again and this time it stayed that way. The patient became unconscious. Another nurse rushed to get the emergency cart and a resuscitation attempt got underway.

This is when something very strange happened. I felt my body being pushed over to the patient's bed. I had no feeling of myself making that decision. I called out his name, facing him, whilst putting both my hands on his shoulders. It seemed as though it was not 'me' doing this. It wasn't a conscious act. I could feel his inner subtle energy through my hands on his shoulders (although I didn't know what it was at the time) and I could feel this energy rebalancing as I remained hovered over him. Once I sensed that his energy was balanced, I somehow knew that all was well with him. Without looking at the heart monitor, I said to the others, 'He's fine.' Then I looked. His heart was beating normally again and his eyes opened. The other two nurses looked at me silently. Never a word was spoken. They departed and I arranged for a doctor review. The man was subsequently sent to a major city hospital for a pacemaker. He survived and went on to live many more years.

This healing episode was quite different to the previous one. In this episode I felt as though my body had been taken over and someone else was in me, using my body to affect the energy of another. Over the following year there were numerous healing episodes, all different. I was always happy that the patients recovered and sometimes the patients were aware and told me and sometimes they weren't. Likewise, sometimes I was aware of the energy transfer and sometimes I wasn't. It was all very hard for me to digest – me of all people, with all these terrible personal problems. At this time I was going through the trauma of a marriage break up and many emotional issues. I was facing. I really understood other people's pain: physical, mental and emotional, because I was going through such pain myself. It was a time when my ego was completely shattered, along with my view of reality. Life was upside down. My nursing work seemed a refuge. To be able to help others with their pain helped me deal with mine.

Later, I recognised that my body could act as a channel for an energy source coming from somewhere outside of me. It seemed to me that the outside energy entered me, coursed through my body and used me to connect with the bodies of the patients in order to alter their energies. Bringing about balance in the subtle energy system allowed these people to avoid death at that particular time. Why those particular people and why me is still a mystery.

After many months of these strange and incomprehensible events happening I couldn't handle it any more. The healing episodes felt a burden. I had so much suffering going on in my own life and I hadn't yet learnt very much about subtle energy. I hadn't yet gone very far in my spiritual search and my personal knowledge was still limited. I did not have the knowledge that I have now. I could not digest what was happening through and to me. It was all so confusing and it was something that I couldn't talk about with anyone as I instinctively knew that no one would understand. So I begged the universe to stop it – and it did stop.

If it has returned since I haven't known about it. I sometimes think it all happened as part of my spiritual education, to open my mind up to the possibility of other realms of existence and other ways of being. It certainly did that. It helped me to not question when subsequent unusual happenings came along as by-products of my deep meditation practice. I took it all as possible then, because I had personally witnessed the impossible. I had witnessed and been part of the transfer of healing energy from one person to the other and in a major life saving way. I couldn't deny the existence of inner subtle energy any longer.

Amit Goswami comments about these sudden healing energies and how difficult they can be for Westerners to accept by saying, "I think that these traumatic effects of raising kundalini (in Western people) are due to the repressed shadow of the Western psyche."[119] I tend to agree with him. Before taking up

119 Goswami, The Visionary, p.238.

the journey of spiritual discovery it is best to begin work on our shadow side (which has been discussed in Chapter 5). However we don't often have this guidance about our progress, especially in the beginning. We tend to learn about a spiritual path in a haphazard fashion. In Eastern traditions people received much more cultural support and education about the possibility of kundalini rising. In our culture it is not talked about, at least not in conservative circles such as when visiting the doctor, as we fear being classified as mentally ill. Modern science still does not acknowledge the existence of subtle energy and its place in healing. In addition, usually our self and spiritual development doesn't happen in a linear fashion. We can go from one level of learning or experience to another without fully understanding what is going on. We do not always have experienced spiritual teachers available to us in the West to help us with these occurrences. It is to be expected that sometimes our inner energies might be unbalanced and the result may be either beneficial to self and others, or not. In the end a good motivation and a good heart becomes the most important thing.

No Scientific Explanation

Ancient cultures encouraged the concept of a balance of inner and outer energy, however we cannot measure subtle energy or even talk about it openly in our Western society, as most people who have not experienced the inner subtle energy are unwilling to believe in its existence. It is very difficult to prove also that inner subtle energy, when blocked, causes disease or injury. The only way that I can prove to myself that subtle energy has a positive effect on my health is by noticing a change in internal energy after meditation and how balanced this makes me feel both physically and mentally. The change in my emotional wellbeing is nothing short of remarkable and I always leave a meditation with a deep feeling of love for self and others. The effect of meditation on the brain and body has been well researched and documented and is no longer in question; however the mechanism for this effect is not so clear. It is only by being sensitive to one's own inner energy that one can determine that there has been an energetic shift in the body and mind. For those people who do not practice sitting meditation but who practice relaxation exercises, tai chi, qigong or yoga, they also report feeling the change in this internal energy after practice.

No doubt one day Western science will have more answers. Currently science is researching black matter, an energy that pervades the universe but which does not have an electrical charge. Scientists are continually finding new types of energy in the universe, however there is still much to be discovered. We may never reach the end of our quest for knowledge about the universe. Personally, I don't need any more explanations about subtle inner energy. I know that my experiences with this energy have expanded my sense of reality to include many other types of reality. They have opened my mind to the possibility of the mind existing in many different realms of experience. I believe, as Tibetan Buddhism advocates, that these mind-altering experiences happen because of shifts in one's subtle energy system and I have learned that certain practices allow that process to happen.

Creativity and Subtle Energy

People who learn to pay attention to different levels of awareness by training themselves in meditation, dreams, music, being quietly in nature, prayer, reflection, creative writing or any other creative or right brain type of activity, find that they begin to be able to access other types of information which seem to come from a different part of the brain or a different level of consciousness. Being aware of and able to feel inner energy is just like this. We have to put our logical thinking brain aside and just 'be' with whatever is happening. Using particular spiritual practices also helps us to become more sensitive to feeling subtle energy.

Our internal subtle energy becomes evident when we foster our creativity – people involved in creative activities are able to feel their energy flow. It becomes a streaming process of creativity, not just an isolated act of creativity, and the creative project may appear to take on a life of its own. It seems to determine its own path and process without conscious brain activity. The activity of creativity, of using the right brain, makes us more sensitive people. If our society becomes too busy for creative activities (and these require one to slow down and turn the mind away from its usual outer busyness) then we deprive people of the opportunity to find and express this other, very subtle side of life. A society that encourages cultural activities, spirituality, dance, literature, music, the arts and difference, goes a long way to encouraging people to be aware of and to be able to express their inner energies.

Just as creative expression allows us to express our inner energies, so repression of inner energies can lead to mental illness and disconnection from self and others. John Sanford in *Dreams and Healing* says that the unconscious is an enormous suppressed energy system which holds much psychic energy and that dreams have the capacity to convey this energy to us.[120] Dreams therefore help the internal energies to flow from the unconscious mind to the conscious mind. This is similar to how any other creative pursuit has an effect on us.

Energetic Component of Feelings and Emotions

Emotions/feelings and thoughts are also forms of energy as they can be isolated to neuronal activity, neurotransmitters and brain activity in general.[121] From a practical point of view, we can feel the energy of power; it is an expansive, energetic, free and strong energy. We can feel the energy of being in control; it is a rigid, secure, contracted, safe, focused and disciplined type of

120 Sanford, p.36.
121 See J LeDoux, *The Emotional Brain.*

energy. We can feel the energy of a broken heart; it is a dull ache or pain right in the chest. We can feel the elation of first love; it is a feeling of high energy and euphoria throughout the body and mind. By becoming more sensitive to the energy inherent in our thoughts and emotions we can begin to watch how they affect self, others and environment. In general, the more energy a feeling or behaviour/habit carries with it, the more we need to pay attention to the roots of that feeling or behaviour as any strong emotion indicates that balance or awareness is lacking.

Gregg Braden puts forward the result of a scientific experiment that shows how the physical shape of DNA can be altered according to the feelings of the subject.[122] Those people trained in experiencing deep love showed a more open and relaxed DNA shape whereas those feeling anger had DNA which was much more tightly configured. This is quite a statement; however we have already heard from scientific research that severe stress can shorten telomeres, the very end of chromosomes and this affects a person's lifespan. In current times all these experiments and ideas are still being put forward. As well as keeping an interest in scientific research about energy, it is good for us to keep an open mind and to try to learn from our own experience of energy within us. When working with the energy of strong emotions we can use the 'observer self' to watch patterns of emotions and behaviour and to watch the energy or force in them. If we can distance ourselves from the thinking active mind without the ego interfering, we stand a better chance of getting to the source of the problem. We all carry many deep and largely unconscious patterns. Jungian dream work, as it works with the unconscious, can help us to find out why some repetitive fears and emotions carry such inner energy. It literally shows us in pictures and symbols the source of our fears and emotions.

122 See G Braden, DNA Can Repair Itself With Feelings, *Whispers from Beyond*, issue 0042, published online, Eaton, Australia, December, 2008, retrieved 30 September 2011, <http://www.whispersfrombeyond.com.au/Newsletters/newsjan08article.htm>

Subtle Energy and Tibetan Buddhist (Tantric) Meditation

In Tibetan Buddhism and other traditions such as Sufism, the gross body (our usual physical body) is said to be undergirded by an energetic body, also called the subtle or illusory body and the consciousness of the person is said to move through this energetic network. Vajrayana Buddhism is a tradition of mind transformation and it is through this work on clearing the gross consciousness by way of working with subtle energy, that Tantra (Vajrayana) is said to be the quickest path to enlightenment or complete awareness. According to Vajrayana Buddhism, subtle energies give our bodies vitality and this subtle energy enters the body through the vehicle of the breath which then flows through nadis or channels throughout the body.

A modern writer, Reginald Ray, in *The Secret of the Vajra World* explains the chakra system by saying that various states of awareness are associated with different parts of the body; for example – strong love and yearning with the heart, speech with the throat, thinking with the head, hunger with the belly and orgasm with the genital area.[123] He equates these areas with the relevant chakras and explains that each of these areas also contain a store of wisdom and compassion. These chakras are linked by energy pathways to the rest of the body and it is along these pathways that consciousness travels by using the prana (subtle energy) as a vehicle. Our awareness then is linked to the subtle energy system and the chakras.

My Own Experiences with Tibetan Buddhist Meditation

If we look at my own story, it might explain how it is possible to understand the energy at a beginning level in Tibetan Buddhist meditation. When I first starting meditating with breath meditations, I began to experience strange feelings. Mostly, in the beginning, I felt body relaxation and a sense of spaciousness

123 Ray, *Secret*, p.232.

but as I progressed to longer breath meditations I began to experience different energy shifts in my body. This often happens to beginning meditators. Sometimes it seemed as though my body was twisting to one side, however when I opened my eyes to look, my body hadn't moved at all. Sometimes my head would feel as though it had become the head of the Buddha, sometimes I felt myself lifted up high into the sky, sometimes I would feel such bliss that I couldn't bear it. Sometimes I would feel energy rising in my spine, moving up to the crown of my head. Sometimes I would feel this vertical energy rising very high up above me in a direct line thousands of miles above and I had the sense of my spine being incredibly straight. Sometimes I would feel as though I couldn't move a muscle in my body, I had become completely immobilised, as though I was coming out of an anaesthetic and couldn't yet move my limbs. Sometimes I sat there for hours without moving. Often I felt myself leave my body, a sense of the body dissolving and myself as just a mist, which also evaporated into an experience of complete fullness and at the same time complete emptiness. Later, I often felt heat rising throughout my body at the completion of the mantra work during practice. These are all experiences of subtle energy moving in the body. They are common enough experiences when one begins on a serious meditation path.

Over time I learnt to accept these occurrences as they came and went. I began to understand that the meditative techniques were altering the energy within and this in turn had an effect on my mind state. At times I felt hugely affected by the majesty of what I was experiencing and until I began reading texts on the meditative experiences of others I worried about what was happening to me. It is unfortunately common in the West to stumble on meditations without the guidance of a spiritual teacher. With time, these initial energetic occurrences settle and change into other more subtle energetic experiences.

In 2002 I was introduced to Tibetan Buddhist meditation through my first teacher of Tibetan Buddhism, a Canadian non-monastic teacher by the name of Catherine Jetsun Yeshe. The first thing that happened energetically when I sat down to meditate in the meditation hall with her leading the meditation was that I felt a distinct tugging on the crown of my head. This was quite painful at first and very scary. Also, later that day, I had a sense of my body shaking that lasted for several hours. By next morning the energies had stabilised but every time I sat down to meditate I felt the pull on the crown chakra very strongly. Over the years this pulling feeling has remained with me. It is often present during my daily meditation and seems particularly associated with devotion to particular meditation masters or particular texts. I have learnt to pay attention to it. I have discovered that often, when I read a meditation text from the Karma Kagyu tradition, just idly reading not meditating, I will feel the tugging on the crown chakra. I cannot explain why that should be except that there is some direct energetic link between these teachings and myself. If I am reading a new text now and this tugging or sense of opening happens, I know that this particular text is important to me.

After I started researching through books and then later with my Buddhist teacher, I began to understand that my experiences of altered energy had been experienced by many meditators over the previous centuries. I learnt that there are a huge number of meditation practices that are concerned with manipulating the vital inner energies with the aim of inducing deeper and subtler states of mind. As I ventured further into Vajrayana practices, I found that most of these practices appeared to work mainly on the energy centres in the upper chakras; mostly at the heart centre or the crown chakra and that the meditations take one to the experience of a higher, deeper or more refined state of consciousness. In Tibetan Buddhism, there are also practices that work with the lower chakras but initially one begins the path with stabilising practices, such as the body and the breath practices, which work on balancing and stabilising the inner energies.

One of my most practiced Tibetan Buddhist meditations, Vajrasattva, is concerned with 'cleansing unwholesomeness from all etheric planes' or clearing energy channels.[124] This particular practice originated from a ninth century meditation master in the Kagyu school of Tibetan Buddhism and has been handed down from that time to this, from master to disciple. The meditation of Vajrasattva talks about channels, veins and nadis, all of which relate to the movement of subtle energy. This practice requires that the meditator visualise a deity completely clear and transparent; the stream of nectar from this being then flows down through the channel in the middle of the body, filling the heart centre and then circulating through all the energy channels of the body. We then visualise the substance cleansing our internal energy channels and leaving the body and dissolving into the earth below. To balance this, we then visualise healing energy filling the body from the base up to the crown of the head. Such visualisations encourage and teach visualisation of the subtle energy pathways and the use of this particular technique to clear energetic blockages.

Whenever I do this particular meditation I feel the sense of the crown chakra tugging/tingling/opening and of there being a communication through this opening. As I type this text I am aware of the tingling as well. Over the years this feeling has never diminished. I have found the Tibetan meditation of Vajrasattva, to be very effective in clearing negative, agitated or confused mind states (as well as headaches!) by leading me gradually to the natural state of still, clear mind. Done on a daily basis it becomes a nourishing and cleansing practice. In many Tibetan Buddhist practices I have noticed the feeling of energy flowing through the central channel, especially if the back is straight and the body is held upright.

Sometimes I use the practice of chanting seed syllables. There is a different one for each chakra. This works over time to open

124 See Friends of the Heart, *The Sadhana of Vajrasattva.*

a chakra or stabilise the inner subtle energy in the body system pertaining to that chakra. Different meditations use different vibrations and seem to affect a different part of the body, if observed carefully. For instance, the syllable LAM, (pronounced Lummmm), if repeated very slowly many times while sitting cross legged on the floor with the back straight, directing the mental attention down to the base of the spine, definitely has the effect of stabilising one's energy within body and mind. One can feel the energy vibrating in that area of the body.

The sadhana of Guru Yoga, which I also use regularly, has a very grounding effect.[125] Sometimes I will experience my voice gradually deepening while I repeat the mantra and I often notice the mantra resonating in, and stabilising, the lower half of my body. The sound of the mantra does this without any conscious effort on my part.

Tibetan Buddhism maintains that by clearing energy channels and chakras, the deep patterns, habits, attitudes, clinging and ignorance which are the basis of karma, are dissolved. The practices of visualisation, mantra and physical posture have this aim. This is the crux of Tibetan Buddhist (Vajrayana) meditation. Meditation focuses on healing the mind through clearing the energy pathways. It does not claim to heal the physical body except perhaps as a by-product of mind healing.

Detection of Subtle Energy has the Capacity to Affect Life

It is important to be able to sense when the energy is out of balance because if it is, then this will affect all our bodily and mental processes. By detecting this change early, we are able to put into place strategies to return our bodies and minds to a state of balance. In this way, subtle energy can be thought of as a warning mechanism. If we sense our mental or bodily energy

---

125 Kalu Rinpoche, *A Rainfall of Blessing: A Guru Yoga*, text from the enthronement celebration booklet to commemorate his reincarnation, Samdrup Sarjay Ling Tibetan Monastery, Sonada, Darjeeling, India, 1993.

becoming restless, angry, irritable or sluggish; then we can take steps to balance ourselves before we feel or become unwell, or we do or fail to do things which we later regret, i.e. we begin to act without awareness. Poor balance of internal energy can lead to a lack of awareness and conversely living with awareness keeps our inner energies in balance. Ultimately the aim of balancing internal subtle energy is to refine the mind state and to achieve healthier physical and psychological states.

Tenzin Wangyal Rinpoche comments with remarkable perception that in Western students of Eastern religions, there is often a separation between the real issues that we have in everyday life and the spiritual life to which we aspire.[126] He suggests that working with our subtle energies, because they bring self-knowledge on such a deep level, can help to bridge this gap between daily life and our spiritual aspirations. He encourages people to do practices like Tibetan sound healing (chanting) to help them to contact and experience their true and authentic nature. As already mentioned, subtle energy is the bridge between body and mind, it is therefore a very appropriate means with which to translate compassionate thought into wise action.

Once we begin working with the inner subtle energies we begin to notice a feeling of having more energy or 'feeling more alive'. Subtle energy is spirit and spirit innervates whatever it touches. As we train in awareness of subtle energy and begin to feel its flow, we develop an inner strength and power that we can't accomplish with thought alone. It translates thought into action. This is the hidden power of subtle energy – it can energise and balance our whole day.

126 Tenzin Wangyal, *Tibetan Sound*, p.ix.

Sound

Sound affects the body by its vibration and energy. If we listen to outer sounds we feel the vibratory sound patterns flowing through our body; if we create the sounds ourselves through our voice, we can feel the effect on the particular part of the body where the sound resonates. Sound is a form of energy which can deeply heal.

According to Tenzin Wangyal Rinpoche in *Tibetan Sound Healing* our spiritual search is a deep longing to know ourselves and to be authentic. He teaches chanting of five seed syllables, OM, AH, HUNG, RAM, DZA, whilst focusing on the feeling experience in the chakra that the sound relates to. Certain pure sound can alter our minds and energy balance to return us to an inner purity or space and a sense of completion, just as we are. Experiencing natural mind is like the experience of 'coming home'.

During meditation practice I have used Tibetan Buddhist mantras, focussed on the sound of a singing bowl being struck, and chanted seed syllables whilst focussing on specific chakras of the body. I have found these three methods to have profound effects. No doubt there are many other equally valuable sound practices.

Body Work and Meditative Movement

Body work is said to involve manipulation of the body and its bioelectrical energy fields. By moving the body in specific positions we cause certain energy meridians to come into alignment so that energy can flow more easily through them and through any blockages along their path. According to Amit Goswami, the aim of practices like tai chi, martial arts and yoga is to gain awareness of and to unite the physical body with the energetic body in our consciousness and to connect that consciousness with the consciousness of the brain or the ego. In other words, we are aiming to integrate all aspects of our being through direct experience of it.[127]

Qigong is an ancient Chinese art that teaches feeling and moving subtle energy for the purposes of health and healing. The practice of qigong claims to activate the vital energy and to move stagnated energy through the subtle energy pathways of the body. It regulates and replenishes our body's energy system. It has been termed the art and science of Chinese energy healing. In China, qigong is practiced for good health and longevity. Medical qigong is also offered in Chinese hospitals. When we have practiced yoga, qigong or tai chi for any length of time with mindfulness, we will begin to notice the feeling of energy or tingling in the fingertips and changes in feelings in and around the whole body at the completion of the set or routine. Often we will feel more peaceful and a general sense of balance, stability and wellbeing. People report feeling calmer, clearer and more energised while feeling more still, refreshed and having a sense of being grounded – as though our feet are in solid connection with the floor. The theory is that certain physical movements encourage the flow of subtle energy through the body.

It is also said that the exaggerated intention or the mindfulness placed on each slight movement in these practices helps the practitioner to be more aware of the energy flow. It is not difficult to demonstrate this even with people who don't do martial arts, body work or movement meditation. We have only to hold the open palms facing and apart, relax them and then be aware of the sensations in the hands as we move them slowly together and then move them slowly apart again. If we pay attention we will soon feel the energy currents flowing in and between the hands.

Breath Work (Meditation)

The yogis of India used breath practices to alter their internal energies which then affected their ability to experience many different states of consciousness. The breath is intimately linked with the mind which is why so many meditations are breath based.

127 Goswami, *The Visionary*, p.233.

In a different way, Tenzin Wangyal Rinpoche talks about using attention to the breath and specific movements of the body to harness and move the internal winds (subtle energy) so that we can recognise our natural mind.[128] The nine breathings of purification, which uses a combination of alternate nostril breathing and visualisation, is another method advocated by this particular meditation master. This practice has some similarity to the yogic alternate nostril breathing and has the ability to change the mind state and energy very quickly.

Tantric/Yogic/Vajrayana Practices

These practices focus solely on the energy underlying the body, mind and emotions. According to Tantra, the emotions have their origin in the energy winds of the subtle/energetic body. The energy wind is also closely associated with consciousness and the more subtle the energy wind, the more subtle the state of consciousness. Tantric practices then, aim to control subtle energy in order to refine consciousness (mind) and emotions. The particular deity practices that I have used with effect are Vajrasattva, Sakyamuni Buddha, Green Tara, Chenresig, Mandala Offering, Guru Yoga and Vajrapani. There are many other deity practices, each one affecting one's subtle energy in a slightly different way. We tend to settle with the meditation that affects our particular energy in a beneficial way.

Meditation is contained in all of the above categories, which is why meditation is so remarkable. Meditation affects body, subtle energy and mind, it is an all inclusive practice. Depending on the practice, it can incorporate meditative body work, breath work, sound, prayer, ritual and visualisation.

Intention, or doing an activity with complete focus, creates awareness which helps us to feel or experience energy flow. People also report feeling group energy in the room where

128 See Tenzin Wangyal Rinpoche, *Awakening the Sacred Body,* Hay House Publishers, USA, 2011.

everyone is doing the same activity. I have noticed this particularly with meditation groups. The combined energy of the people in the room who are of the same mindset is greater than the individual energies combined. People report feeling the energy as stronger or more powerful and therefore it is often easier for people to begin experiencing subtle energy within such a supported group situation. Practicing with a teacher also helps learning meditators to feel the changes in subtle energy more easily than if they practice alone.

Balancing our Energy Generally

In my latter years I have understood the need for mental and physical stability. Like other people, I can be totally in a daydream, without focus, or alternatively I can be racing around doing everything at once with a very active mind. Neither of which are very mindful! To keep myself balanced (earthed), I have learnt to balance my personality with several practices or activities. Every person can work this out for themselves.

Gaining knowledge of the elements of earth, fire, air, water and space and how, in different proportions, they are part of our personal psychological makeup, is useful information to have. When we are feeling out of balance at any particular time, this knowledge of our elemental parts, can help us to see what we need to do to bring ourselves into a more balanced energetic state. Tenzin Wangyal Rinpoche, in *Healing with Form, Energy and Light*, has written an excellent chapter on "relating oneself to the elements".[129] This process of balancing internal energy begins with recognising that we feel 'out of sorts'. The energy may be too fast and restless or it may be sluggish. Both can affect how we feel and how we interact with others.

---

129 Tenzin Wangyal Rinpoche, *Healing with Form, Energy and Light*, Snow Lion Publications, New York, 2002, pp.12-26.

A short practice which I find particularly effective and which can be used whilst standing during the day, is the repeated mantra, LAM (pronounced Luuuuumm), said out loud for several minutes while placing the attention on the pelvic area. This quickly brings me back to a feeling of being centred down in the base chakra. Another very good practice for some people is pulling out weeds or gardening – contact with the earth can be very grounding and energy balancing. There are many more such practices to be found in daily life.

For many of us in Western society our energy will tend to be in the upper chakras as we are so mentally active and mentally stimulated. Therapies such as foot massage, progressive muscle relaxation from the waist down, repeating an affirmation such as 'take your time' over and over, and sexual activities which bring the energy down, all have an effect. Quite often if I can feel the inner energies too much in my head, I will simply stop, stand or sit still for a moment and direct my attention to my feet and legs, keeping the spine straight and breathing abdominally. Lately, I have been doing pelvic floor exercises and this helps too! Any activity which directs the attention downwards will work. For most of us living in our technological world it is most important to work on balancing the base chakra before working with any other. We need first to build a solid base. We can't step out and take charge of thoughts, emotions or actions if we are not grounded and strong within ourselves. This type of energy balancing is so important for us to do.

Physical activity such as a daily walk also appears to have the effect of moving subtle energy around the body. We feel more alive and fresher afterwards. I suspect that exercise works in a general way on the subtle energy system, moving it through the channels and keeping the 'plumbing open'. If we can do this exercise outside in the fresh air we will be getting the additional benefit of receiving energy from the environment, from plants, air/wind, the sea and the earth. We have all experienced the effect of a brisk early morning walk on improving our mood. A mood is a mixture of emotion and thought. Somehow the energy of exercise moves this stagnant negative energy along, and causes the release of circulating hormones and endorphins that make us feel good.

Tenzin Wangul Rinpoche remarks that a secure home, a healthy relationship and a solid job can also help to ground us and are good for counteracting anxiety. [130] He adds that certain physical postures (i.e. yoga) and developing focus and concentration in meditation, also ground the energy. He recommends Guru Yoga practice to bring the energy down.

Relationship can inadvertently help to balance one's subtle energies if one chooses a partner with a complementary type of energy. If one tends to be a person who has a very active mind, then to be in an intimate relationship with a person who lives more in the lower energy centres of stability and groundedness, can be good and balancing for both people. We know for ourselves that our energies in an intimate relationship overlap. We are affected by each other's moods and actions. We can feel the type of energy that is flowing out of our partner on a particular day. Relationships of all types are energy exchanges but particularly intimate relationships. From this we can see that the more we work on improving the healthy flow of our own energies, the more our partner will be positively affected by that also, and vice versa. Relationships between parents and children are very close and emotionally bonded relationships. Here it is very easy to see the energetic connection. In the same way that we have energetic bonds with close people, so we have energetic bonds with all people on the planet. Many people are influenced by our choices, words and acts, not just those in close proximity to us. Thoughts, words and actions are energy forms not limited to time and place.

130 Tenzin Wangyal, *Healing with Form*, p.14.

The Rejuvenating Energy of the Life Force

How can we begin to build a positive balance of energy instead of depleting it? We know that rest and sleep help replenish the body's gross stores of energy but how do we replenish our subtle inner energy stores? Rest, happy and healthy company, a good diet, being outside in nature and a pleasant environment certainly help but we can also use spiritual practices to replenish our life force. For some people, creative activities such as art or music also help them to achieve this feeling of richness or replenishment. We need to use practices or activities which make us feel more positive, more alive, and clearer and nourished. I have a dear friend who practices tai chi every morning and always seems to have abundant energy and another good friend who teaches qigong and yoga and similarly, she also has a life of positivity and engagement with the world.

Meditation has always done this for me. If I miss my meditation for a few days I sense that some part of me needs feeding. Some part of me is not getting what it needs to survive and I sense that my energies are becoming depleted. It is as though I need to plug myself in to be recharged every day! In effect I am plugging into the universal source: natural mind, pure consciousness, God, Tao, the divine, universal energy; whatever one calls it. There are many ways that we can do this recharging, each person will know instinctively what is necessary to keep this energetic balance for them, the important thing is to make time for it.

* * *

Subtle energy is the link between body and mind and as such affects both. It is the vehicle which can help us to translate thought and aspiration into the action of our daily lives. Working with subtle energy in the body is very important in helping us to be physically healthier, mentally more aware and emotionally more stable. Learning how to work with our internal energies helps us to broaden our experiences of consciousness and this knowledge is intimately associated with our degree of awareness in general. Learning techniques which allow us to contact our subtle energy also help us to return to our source of spiritual nourishment; our own true nature – our natural mind, which is a great source of wholeness or completion for us. Awareness of subtle energy leads to greater 'aliveness' – we begin finally to truly live and embrace life. We are then able to use all of life's experiences as opportunities on our spiritual path, with a sense of meaning and enjoyment.

CHAPTER SEVEN
AWARENESS IN RELATIONSHIP

Relationships are essentially connections: physical, emotional and energetic. These can include relationships with parents, siblings, colleagues, children, friends, acquaintances, strangers, relatives, partners and animals. We are also constantly in a relationship with ourselves. Relationships give us the experience of belonging and encourage us to develop skill and awareness. They teach us how to love. How we manage a relationship is important to our survival on this planet and to our quality of life while we are here. Most of us find intimate or long term relationships the most challenging to maintain over time and so this chapter focuses on those. Intimate relationships very quickly bring us face-to-face with our own personal issues.

Nowadays, there is much more information and knowledge about the world and about relationships than ever before, however people continue to fall into the same problems of relating. What we learn in childhood – and our personalities –

are difficult to change. It is amusing (and frustrating) to observe that we often attract partners who mirror who we are, rather than partners who we (ideally) want. We may not understand this, however, until some years have passed and we have lost our 'rose-coloured glasses'.

One thing we can be sure of is that our interaction with others will always change both of us to some degree. We are all interdependent.

Awareness of the Heart

Unless we have experienced the emotions of the heart we are unable to experience the full range and depth of our humanity. Love is a heart quality and it is through being loved that we learn to love. It is through our most important first contact with our mother or primary caregiver, that we discover the bond and attachment to another being. During our growing years our social environment moulds us as well and we evolve in our own right as individuals, separate from our caregivers. As we progress into adulthood our changing hormonal balance again steers us in the direction of love, attachment and matters of the heart.

In Western society we associate the heart with the qualities of love, empathy, grieving, loss, compassion and joy. We talk about having 'a heavy heart' if we are sad, 'a broken heart' if we have been hurt in a love relationship, and 'no heart' if we have no compassion for others. Our society attributes to the heart the qualities of feeling. Eastern cultures consider the heart to have the additional qualities of wisdom, power and intelligence. In Eastern philosophy, the term 'awakening the heart' refers to developing compassion, love and joy through practices such as meditation. The Mahayana school of Buddhism specifically focuses on the development of heart qualities such as wisdom, discrimination, generosity, helping others and compassion.[131] The meditation practice of Tonglen specifically teaches the heart

131 R Ray, *Indestructible Truth*. Shambhala, Boston, 2002, pp.311-330.

skill of giving love and taking away suffering. This practice, as well as many others, is repeated over and over again until the meditator begins to experience the heart quality arising and flowing from the heart. The heart quality of wisdom is considered most important in helping or loving others wisely and with discrimination.

In recent Western scientific research we see a discipline developing which espouses the idea that the heart has its own intelligence. HeartMath[132] is an organisation that is involved in such research. Scientists are discovering that there are cells embedded in the heart which act exactly as the brain cells in the brain do, and that the heart and mind share a circuit of neurons, blood supply, nervous innervations, chemicals, hormones and neurotransmitters, which means that they work synchronistically because of the close connection between their parts. What is being suggested is that there is a very close relationship with the heart and the brain/mind. This dual organ system supports the research findings that the heart has its own intelligence. Many of us have noticed during our lives that major decisions are made not just with our logical brains but also with our hearts. In times of silence and reflection we may feel the qualities of wisdom and intuition as coming from the heart. HeartMath research is actually proposing that the heart provides guidance and intelligence.

For thousands of years, spiritual traditions have been aware of the power of the heart when joined with the mind. Meditation particularly aims not just to train the mind but also to open the heart, to increase its positive qualities. Working to increase heart qualities has been shown to increase well-being and happiness, something that we readily experience in our everyday lives.[133] For many of us, our first experience of an awakening of the power and the qualities of the heart comes with our first experience of conscious relationship. This may be with the beginning of a

132 HeartMath <http:// www.heartmath.org>
133 See State Govt of Victoria, Better Health Channel.

close/intimate relationship, the birth of one's children or any other strong relationship. Ironically, it is often not until we have suffered with a broken heart or other major loss that we are capable of understanding at a very deep level the feelings of others who are experiencing the same fate. Relationship then, is a universal and everyday opportunity for learning about and practicing the development of positive heart qualities.

Awareness of Self in Relationship

Why are We in a Particular Relationship?

We may have heard it mentioned in self-help literature that we create our own relationships or that we choose a relationship with a person with opposite qualities, to 'balance' us; or that we draw people to us who mirror to us our own failings or psychological gaps. Some authors of quantum physics literature seem to have a distinct leaning towards the fact that we do create our own reality because of the fact that we and everything in the universe are made of the same basic matter and space.[134] The laws of particle physics show us that sub-microscopic particles behave in amazing ways and that every particle/wave has interdependency with every other particle/wave.[135]

The great spiritual traditions of the East have always maintained the existence of this link or interdependence between all living things and they base this knowledge on mystical experiences which show that we are all one. There are also modern experiments which show that we can influence other people at great distances through our thoughts, showing that people are not as separate from others as we may have been led to believe. Carl Jung maintained that it our unconscious, projected onto the beloved other, which causes passionate attraction.[136] There is

134 Goswami, *The Visionary*, pp. 43-60.
135 Goldberg & Blomquist, p.66.

136 Goswami, *The Visionary*, p.117.

much published material on this issue of just how much influence we have on attracting people towards us.

Luck, Destiny, Manifestation or Synchronicity?

Yet there is another aspect to the creation of relationships that appears driven by intuition or chance. Often there is a great synchronicity to the meeting of two people. People say that they just happened to be 'in the right place at the right time' or that it was pure luck. Buddhists would call this type of meeting karma (which ultimately is still self-determined); New Age people would perhaps call this the power of the Divine or Essence working through us; Jung claimed it was the Self guiding us towards wholeness through archetypal processes being activated in the unconscious.[137] Authors such as Ian Gawler and others believe in manifestation which he describes as 'the ability to bring into reality the things you genuinely and reasonably need in your life'.[138]

Clairvoyants appear to see into the future but they would explain that this life we live is already present in us even though we are unaware of it – it is present in our energy field before we manifest it. The clairvoyant claims to see the future in our energy field. And then there is the New Age view that if a relationship does not assist us to fulfil our life's purpose (spiritual/self development) then it won't be successful. Certainly some unconscious method of meeting and choosing is at play. Could this feeling that we have no control over our relationships simply be because we are unaware of our part in choosing and meeting people?

We will all have different needs incorporated into our finding of a partner as we are all different. For myself, I distinctly remember an intuitive feeling that I had done as much self-development work alone and in meditation as I could and that now it was time to find a relationship to further my learning. I had been living the single life for thirteen years whilst the

137 A Storr, *The Essential Jung*, Fontana Press, London, 1998, p.414.
138 Storr, pp.423-424.

children were growing up and I had been very conscious during that time of the need to do lots of inner work without the distractions of an intimate relationship. I had many areas of unawareness to work through. It wasn't my choice to be alone; a new relationship simply didn't happen during that time. I do believe that life presents change and opportunity to us at the exact right time, when we are ready for it. I sensed that I was ready to begin learning the lessons of sharing, compromise and unconditional love in a committed relationship – all tough lessons for an independent and sometimes selfish person. A part of me was actually terrified about taking this step.

I had told several friends that I was looking for a male hiking partner when a good nursing friend of mine came across a single man during her work day who also liked to hike. She tells the story that when she met this man and began talking with him, an image of my face flashed into her mind. She checked with both of us, telling me how nice she thought he was, and instigated an exchange of phone numbers. We were both quite cautious, and as I remember, we spent our first meeting on a tough, four-hour hike with very little conversation. It was this man's 'presence' or energy, however, which made a lasting impression on me and fortunately, this seemed to be mutual. It is possible that luck, destiny, manifestation, synchronicity and karma all played a part in our meeting.

Our Expectations

When people attempt to meet a partner by first making a list of their ideal partner's qualities, often this doesn't seem to work. Some people have huge and unrealistic expectations about what a prospective partner should embody. Unfortunately the search is often for someone of movie star appearance, a big house and a scintillating intellect! And when we are looking, we never think about the possibility of having to give up things and to compromise and adapt to the other.

Our search for a partner, if we do it without awareness is all too often led by the ego. The ego has very strict criteria about what it wants, but often the ego is attracted to the wrong partner – it chooses a partner who will uphold its standards of appearance, similarity to us, status, education and financial security. Certainly having some things in common helps us to bond however, the most important qualities that we need to be looking out for in a prospective partner are the heart qualities of love and kindness, both for him/herself and others. All other traits and qualities will be secondary to this and can be accommodated. As the saying goes, it's what is on the inside that counts.

This is not to say that in a relationship we give up what is important for our own-wellbeing. We need to be quite realistic about what we need for ourselves as well. Some of the most cherished people in our lives are those who are happy and who make others happy. For this reason it is important to keep up interests and activities which make us happy. Sometimes a new relationship with a person having different interests may question the time we spend on our interests but it is vital that we continue to nurture those things that feed our soul. We all know that certain activities - sport, family time, social engagements, being out in nature, the cinema, motor bike riding - can make us feel good. A respectful relationship does not seek to dominate or control these activities of the other.

Our personal happiness is a very necessary base on which we build the ability to spread our contentment and well-being to others. By each partner allowing the other his/her necessary independence, ironically the relationship can become stronger, as such trust generates deep respect. The degree of independence is something to be negotiated and for each couple this balance will be different. As always, respectful communication of needs is the key.

We will all be aware of how our deepest anxieties, as well as how we have communicated in the past, play a part in every negotiation we have with our partner. It is difficult, to say the least, to speak with our mind focused in the present, as so much of what we say is based on past experience. How often do we find sharp words flying out of our mouths automatically as though it is some stranger speaking? We can be horrified sometimes at what we say without thinking. It is a great help if we can begin to work with the deep motivations which lie beneath why we say and react the way that we do. Personally, I have found Jungian dream analysis to delve into these deep layers with better results than other types of therapy. We cannot expect to have a good relationship unless we have contacted and become aware of our own 'missing' parts.

Becoming More Psychologically Aware

We struggle with all types of relationships if we have not first learnt some degree of self-awareness or not learnt a little about self-responsibility for our actions and lives. Carl Jung wrote that we need to become more aware of our inner psychological workings saying, "The psychological rule says that when an inner situation is not made conscious, it happens outside as fate".[139] To translate; he is saying that any shortcomings that we have will appear to us in life's situations and in the people we meet. What we regard as 'fate' is simply this process.

And Eknath Easwaran speaks about the importance of self-knowledge. "To know others, you do not have to go and knock on four billion separate doors. Once you have seen your real Self, you have seen the Self in all. It makes it easy to understand and to forgive, and very difficult to quarrel. All of life springs from the same root. The Self in each of us is one and the same."[140]

139 See Jung, *Collected Works*, Christ.

140 See E Easwaran, *Words to Live By*, Blue Mountain Meditation Center, California, USA, 2005. <http://www.easwaran.org >

Romantic Love

Eawaran talks about romantic love as having replaced religion as the means of finding and satisfying the needs of the soul. He says that we look to the other idealised person to fill our psychological gaps instead of looking inwards to see how we can best complete ourselves. He says: "Romance must, by its very nature, deteriorate into egotism. For romance is not a love that is directed at another human being: the passion of romance is always directed at our own projections, our own expectations, our own fantasies. In a very real sense, it is a love not of another person, but of ourselves."[141]

Robert Johnson in *The Psychology of Romantic Love*[142] has also written an excellent book on this topic. Initially it is common for relationships to begin out of mutual need. If there is no reward or benefit for the person giving love to another then the love soon dies.

The Role of Our Ego

The role our ego plays in how we relate to another is often something that we are unaware of. Our ego is the part of us that directs us to do things; like an inner voice. It wants things and situations to be only how we expect or wish them to be, which may, at times, directly oppose what is helpful for a loving relationship between two people. The ego is never satisfied, is basically self-centred and nothing is ever quite good enough. The demands of the ego come from our previous conditioning (our beliefs, opinions, preferences, how we like things done). The ego doesn't like differences and won't feel comfortable with a partner who challenges us to be different.

The ego only allows limited choices within its framework of what is safe for us and what is not. When we react from ego, we

141 See Easwaran, *Words to Live By.*
142 See Johnson, *The Psychology of.*

become reactive, defensive and we use conditioned responses. Ego makes it difficult for us to accept responsibility for what we do. This makes a relationship challenging. When we relate from the ego we feel safe but constricted and generally we feel unloving and focused in our past history. Whereas when we relate from our heart we generally feel more loving and are more focused in the present moment.

First Develop Awareness of Our Relating Patterns

Relationship can be one of the most frustrating and difficult teachers we can ever have. It can bring so much heartbreak and pain when things go wrong. Relationship is a mirror; remember the concept of 'as within, so without' and the following quote by African-American novelist James Baldwin: "One can only face in others what one can face in oneself."[143] The health of our relationships with other people is a direct indication of the progress we are making in our relationship with all the different aspects of ourselves. For most of us this is a lifelong task.

When a relationship is terminated by the other person the sense of rejection and loss of confidence may seem almost too much to bear. Most of us feel unloved and inadequate when this happens and we may seek solace in the company of friends who boost our self-esteem with encouragement. Others may not have received, or asked for, any support and may have enter their next relationship with unresolved feelings that can fester. These need to be sorted through if we wish to have a better relationship next time. Counselling and psychotherapy are good tools for exploring the roots of feelings associated with relationship so that we will be armed with more knowledge about ourselves in order to proceed with life.

---

143 See J Baldwin, *Notes of a Native Son*, Beacon Press, USA, 1984.

Why Did I Marry You?

The reasons why we are attracted to someone else in a love relationship have been described as 'chemistry' but in fact they are much more than that. In Warwick Hartin's wonderful little book *Why Did I Marry You?* he talks about the three essential components of a marriage being the social, the sexual and the psychological, with the psychological being the most difficult to understand.[144] The explanation for this lies partly in the partner and partly in our family or origin. According to Hartin, the experiences of our family of origin shape our emotional needs and our choice of a partner. Some people may choose in their own marriage to correct what they see as deficiencies in their parents' marriage and there is danger here of over-correction or moving too far in the opposite direction. Some people choose a partner who will make up for what they have missed in childhood. Some people unconsciously choose a partner with whom they repeat their childhood experiences, so that they have an opportunity to relive and hopefully correct, their experience as an adult. Some people may choose a partner who plays second fiddle to their own childhood loyalties to one or other parent.

Psychologically then, it seems that we choose a partner who is able to play the matching role to the role we need to play. All this is quite unconscious of course and most people enter into relationships totally unaware of the emotional currents that run under the psychological surface. Because both parties are unaware of the original problems, they really don't understand what their relationship problems are about. Warwick Hartin says marriage is an unconscious process which gives us another chance to resolve difficulties from earlier in our lives. He says, "Although some couples might be mismatched in other ways, from the point of view of their psychological or personality development, marital partners choose each other with exquisite accuracy."[145]

144 W Hartin, *Why Did I Marry You?* Hill of Content, Melbourne, 1988.

145 Hartin, p.39.

Meditation as a Help

The beauty of meditation and other spiritual work is that it shows us glimpses of life without the influence of the ego. In meditation, we may experience higher states of consciousness in which we experience a sense of no ego and no boundaries so that all is experienced as one. As a result of experiencing that state, we know that all beings are interrelated and that if I hurt you, then I am also hurting me. From experiencing these states we experientially learn this, but putting that knowledge into practice is another thing. Author Amit Goswami warns that meditative insights don't immediately improve relationships but that they provide material to work with – they can be a stepping stone to further self-development.[146]

The other main way that meditation helps us with relationships is that it encourages us to learn one-pointed attention (mindfulness). This skill is invaluable in relationships. Giving our complete attention to another is a precious gift. When we are fully present in the moment, listening with our full attention, we are much more likely to be able to respond appropriately to the other and with kindness because we are much more aware of what we are saying, thinking and doing. This is awareness training in action.

In my own life, when there is an issue between myself and another person, I notice that my immediate reaction is to relate that issue to how it is going to affect me (my ego). My ego immediately asks, 'Will this diminish me in any way? Am I going to lose out? Will my pride be hurt? Will it stop me doing what I want to do? Will I have to give anything up?' And a very important one: 'Will I lose control?' 'Me. Me. Me...' Then awareness kicks in after this immediate reaction. The power of awareness is in its ability to temper and slow the ego's assessment and reaction.

146 Goswami, *The Visionary*, p.254.

The next step after learning to be more aware is the notion of choice. We may choose to change our reaction, to stay the same, to be less emotional, to drop the need to be right or any other possible reactions. The point is that we have some choice. Even if we can't change our reaction or behaviour in the short term, if we persevere and have good intentions, it will gradually soften. It is often not until we look back over the years that we notice the disappearance or softening of some aspect of ourselves. Relationship gives us plenty of opportunities to practice!

Relationship as an Opportunity for Growth

The Mirror Aspect

The close/intimate relationship area of life can bring great joy, great pain and many states in between. Our closest relationships are the ones which will teach us the most about the parts of ourselves that we are not consciously aware of. We can't escape from these long-term relationships once we're in them, in the sense that we can spend an hour or two with a friend being loving and kind, and then go home (to be ourselves again). A partner in a close relationship eventually will see everything that we do; all our peculiarities, insecurities and anxieties. We often can't hide our thoughts either because they show on our faces or loved ones soon learn to decipher our facial expressions. In close relationship there is no escaping exactly how we interact with others. It is mirrored back to us. A partner will often point out to us exactly what we don't want to hear. Our children also seem to have this uncanny ability to know us well and to honestly point out our failings to us.

Undoubtedly we can gain much self-knowledge and experience about many things in life without an intimate relationship. Sometimes it may even be more effective to do this self-development work without the distractions, demands and energy exchange of an intimate relationship. However, because we live within our own filters, it is difficult for us to see what our blocks are – mental, psychological, emotional, sexual and relational. We all have this shadow side as we have seen, which is protective of our self-image. When we are unaware, our ego can make all the decisions.

Many of us never allow another person to see us in all our vulnerability despite living together for many years. There may be hurt areas in us that go too deep or aspects of ourselves or our past of which we are ashamed. If we don't learn to work with the integration of this hidden or shadow side into our psyches we will be unable to progress. By working on our shadow side we become willing to see the part that we play in attracting certain relationship issues into our lives and the huge part that our shadow aspects play in how we interact in relationship.

The Creation of a Stronger Unit

Close/intimate relationship is the perfect bridge between spirit and earth. We are forced to look for ways which extend us and make us grow, in the interests of harmony between two people who choose to live together. We all of a sudden have someone else's opinion and likes/dislikes to consider. We can no longer do exactly as we please. We become a unit of two people who are searching for ways that will not only help us to grow as individuals but also that will help the relationship grow as a form of energy in its own right. If we flunk some of the lessons that relationship as teacher is bound to throw our way, we know that our partner won't give up on us and we provide the same base for our partner, providing the relationship allows us our self-respect. It is worth remembering that people enter relationships for many different reasons. For instance, it is also possible that a relationship won't allow the two people to grow but it will keep them safe. It is said that the sign of a successful relationship is one in which both people consider it to be so. We cannot judge the success or otherwise of another's relationship.

Thoughtfulness

For a relationship to survive and grow it requires more than just commitment. There is also a need for the individuals to become 'we centred' rather than 'me centred'. This is where the concept of thoughtfulness comes in. The quality and power of thoughtfulness in relationship should not be underestimated. It is a heart quality, closely related to the teaching of loving kindness in Buddhism.[147] In modern times we don't hear the word very frequently, but thoughtfulness, or thinking about the needs and wants of another when it results in action, can bring happiness to the giver and create reciprocal feelings of love and thoughtfulness in the receiver.

Thoughtfulness in action is an incredibly powerful and positive boost to a relationship. It is a quality that teaches by example. I have found the best way to get me to improve my behaviour and attitude is when my husband (often unintentionally) models a new behaviour to me. After he has brought me countless cups of morning coffee in bed over the years, gone without milk in the morning so that there is milk left for my breakfast and listened to my fears and complaints with unwavering support, I begin to see the connection between thoughtfulness and a good relationship. Then I try it out. I have a long way to go. As parents, we develop thoughtfulness instinctively for our children but that quality may not carry over into our other relationships. Thoughtfulness in a committed long-term love relationship is a quality well-worth cultivating.

Obligation, Mutual Dependence and Need Fulfilment

Being obligated towards a partner, depending on him or her for certain things and having our partner meet some of our needs are perfectly acceptable aspects of a good relationship. Additionally, having some independence in a relationship, where

147 See Friends of the Western Buddhist Order, *Metta: The Practice of Loving Kindness*, Windhorse Publications, Birmingham, 2000.

both partners are free to follow their individual interests and life path, needs to be present. In modern times we are well aware of issues of gender equality and independence, however a long-term relationship over time may soften our black and white way of looking at these issues as relationship requires us to develop flexibility. Once we commit to a close/intimate relationship we become two and not one, and so, for the survival of the relationship, this brings the obligation to care for each other. In this sense we have a reciprocal obligation.

We also need a sense of belonging and caring, and we benefit from having our emotional, sexual and other needs met. We cannot meet the need for intimate touch, deep connection and affection, alone. Our survival and our enjoyment of life are enhanced if we can share the day-to-day responsibilities and the happy times with a trusted other. Once people begin to recognise the importance the other person has in their lives, then an attachment or bond grows which often carries with it a degree of dependence. Mutual dependence means that each person becomes emotionally important to the other, and fulfilling some of the needs of the other person is an important aspect of what keeps people together. There are of course others ways to obtain affection for those without partners, such as through family, friends and animals and these other ways can be sufficient for us to lead contented, fulfilled lives.

Awareness of Intimacy and Solitude Issues in Relationship

Intimacy and our ability to be intimate with others is reflected in the way that we experience our own sense of self. We need to be able to trust, accept and be with ourselves before we can trust, accept and be with another. Bon Tibetan master, Tenzin Wangyal Rinpoche, puts it another way. He says that in order to have the ability to share our personal space with another, we first need to be able to contact our own inner space.[148] We need to clear,

148 Tenzin Wangyal, *Tibetan Sound*, p.52

connect with and recognise spaciousness within ourselves. This work of learning how to be comfortable with our own essence first, is very important.

I love this poem taken from Stephanie Dowrick's book *Intimacy and Solitude*.[149] It talks about self-trust and how one needs to be able to be with, or accept oneself as though we are our own best friend. It probably appeals to me because, in the 1960s, children spent a great deal of time playing and being outside – sitting on steps and fences! When families were larger and houses smaller, being outside alone gave us moments of solitude from siblings and parents.

'Come sit down beside me,
I said to myself,
And although it doesn't make sense,
I held my own hand
As a small sign of trust
And together I sat on the fence.'

Michael Leunig, '*Sitting on the Fence*'

What is Intimacy Then?

Intimacy is closeness between two people which comes about when they can trust each other enough to share openly their inadequacies, failings and embarrassing moments, as well as their joys and happy moments. Intimacy grows from doing little things together. Intimacy also begins from the inside – from being able to accept oneself through all one's own failings and joy. Intimacy is a celebration of our humanity in all its forms. Intimacy generates further trust and acceptance in self and in the other. Without intimacy and trust we will not be able to resolve conflict as we won't trust ourselves or the other with our strong feelings. Intimacy means tuning into how someone else

149 S Dowrick, *Intimacy and Solitude*, William Heinemann, Australia. 1992, p.1.

sees the world and accepting them for that. It is a powerful way of breaking our identification with our ego if we can step into someone else's reality.

Then there is solitude.

At particular times we may require more solitude than intimacy and at other times we may require more intimacy than solitude. We need to be aware of our reaction to issues of solitude and intimacy. How we deal with one will often reflect to us how we deal with the other. Do we become anxious if left alone for too long or are we someone who can't wait to get home and be alone? Some of us find environmental and social stimulation drains our energy while others of us find not enough stimulation, or too much quiet, frightening. Most of us are somewhere in between and there may be a sense of needing balance in both areas. We are all biologically, psychologically and genetically different which makes us prefer one to the other. Additionally, there are many ways of feeling and expressing solitude and intimacy. It is an excellent thing that we are not all the same.

Solitude can be very nourishing and renewing. It can allow us to daydream, allow new ideas to come up, allow us to process the happenings of our lives and allow creative material to arise without the energy or the presence of others to distract us. We can let go of the image that we portray to the world, we can lose our egos. I love to be alone for long periods of time and after that I am happy again to interact with others. If I don't get my alone time I can become short-tempered and difficult to live with and the joy in life goes. My inner life nourishes me for my outer life.

We all need to reflect on these issues for ourselves and how we negotiate this balance in a relationship - between getting too close, too often and growing too far away - is a complicated dance that is forever changing. There is no easy answer because our needs for closeness and aloneness are constantly changing. We need to be flexible in this matter. We will not always be able to have exactly the amount of solitude or intimacy that we wish for and we may be required to give and take so that ultimately, both partners are mostly satisfied. This issue is basic to two people getting along well over a long period of time.

Awareness of our Sexual Selves in Relationship

A Very Powerful Energy

A sexual relationship is one component of intimacy, although for some people, sex can happen with no intimacy at all. In a close/ intimate relationship, sex serves many functions depending on our stage of life and our sexual experience. When we are young the desire for sexual gratification can be huge. We can almost compare it to the roaring of a baby waiting to be fed. It is an energy that cannot be denied no matter what the consequences. It is an incredibly strong biological energy which exists on one of the deepest levels of our being and is a strong survival instinct for the human race.

When we are young, and even when we are older, we may have little control over our sexual impulses and desires. Once the flood gates have been opened there may be no stopping the need. Our morals may fly out the window and should there be a moral conflict, we may have little control. In the wise words of Damaris Parker-Rhodes:

"Our love and sex lives are only as mature as we are and not more so – Therefore mistakes and betrayals must happen." [150]

Sexual betrayals and mistakes can happen in people of any age. A large factor is the degree of awareness we have of ourselves (of who we are) in a sexual relationship. This type of awareness is a process like any other. Spiritual, psychological or academic learning is not always enough to teach us how to

150 Dowrick, p.247.

control our sexual, emotional energy responsibly. It comes with trial and error for most of us and we may learn painfully from the consequences, hurting ourselves and others as we learn.

Sex as a Changing Experience

Sexual desire can catapult us out of all our previous conditioning. We don't recognise the person that we've become and sometimes our desire can be all consuming. We feel a one-ness or complete unity when we have sex with the other person. We feel our boundaries of self dissolving and a merging into one occurring. With the addition of intense pleasure, it is no wonder that we all crave this escape from ourselves and this opportunity for a transcendent experience. In the beginning we look upon our partner as a god or a goddess, that they can create this amazing state for us. Our whole day is charged with this superhuman power or energy. We are huge, all-powerful and all-loving and we don't want to let our partner out of our sight.

As time goes on, we begin to lose that loving energy. The hormones settle. The bliss doesn't last through the day anymore. We stop loving our partner in the way that we did at first. We start to notice things in our partner that we didn't see before; things that we perhaps don't like. As time passes we think that maybe that person has changed; that they aren't a god or goddess after all. Where has the good sex gone? Has that person changed?

Have we made a mistake? What went wrong?

The Mystical Aspect of Sex

In effect, what we have had initially is a spiritual experience that has happened as a by-product of our human need for copulation. Sexual union can be a divine experience, experienced in the earthly realm. It is the experience that meditators crave as well as lovers; this experience of being one with the divine. Sex can be an experience of complete freedom with no boundaries to the self, a sense of nothingness, and huge bliss. The serious meditator can create this mind state alone, without a relationship with another, but then he/she misses out on the physical pleasure, the touch of another and the opportunities for growth which are inherent in a close/intimate relationship. During meditation the meditator experiences intimacy with him/herself and the divine. In effect he/she creates this mind/body state, which is full of energy and yet, strangely enough, there is at the same time, nothing. It is a state of perfection and perfect balance. One wants nothing more. One doesn't want to leave it. But inevitably the meditator also has to come back down to earth and face life as it is.

What happens in the bliss of orgasm and in the higher meditative states, from an energetic point of view, is a free flowing of subtle energy within each person. According to the Eastern traditions, intercourse (or meditation) causes subtle energy to be released from the lower chakra regions of the body. This released energy travels upwards through the energy channels (nadis or meridians) which travel up alongside the spine and up through the crown chakra to produce the state of bliss.[151]

From a Western scientific perspective, neurotheologians D'Aquili and Newberg in their book, *A Mystical Mind*, describe the sensation of intense pleasure/bliss and a sense of union, in both mystical states and orgasm, as being caused by intense simultaneous discharge from both autonomic systems - the sympathetic (arousal system) and the parasympathetic (quiescent system).[152] So it is possible that these experiences are caused by physiological processes in the biology of the brain set off by certain tactile stimulation, resulting in orgasm in the case of sex, or caused by ritual plus repetitive aural stimulation such as mantra, in the case of meditation. Undoubtedly, there is more to unravel about these experiences yet.

---

151 Thubten Yeshe, *The Bliss of Inner Fire*, Wisdom Publications, Boston, 1998, pp.148-149.
152 D'Aquili & Newberg, p.90.

An accomplished meditator can create bliss by mind training. Unfortunately this achievement in meditation is not easily won, or more people would be meditating regularly. It usually requires consistent, dedicated practice. In the Eastern traditions, methods such as Buddhist Tantra provide instructions on how the experienced meditator can control and move sexual energy within the body.[153] These were taught only to experienced meditators and the secrets were closely guarded.

Generally, mystical practices take a lot of hard work to experience, whereas sex is relatively freely available. The catch is that we need another consenting person, preferably in an intimate relationship of trust, to have good sex. If we don't want to go to the trouble of years of learning and practicing mind training and spiritual practices, then we need to go to the trouble of creating a good and intimate relationship with another human being. Of course, there is nothing stopping us going for both mystical experiences and good sex. Some practices in Tantric Buddhism included both. Whichever path/s we end up travelling, it seems that bliss and ecstasy are not obtained easily or lightly and they are both powerful experiences to be treated with respect.

Sex and Intimacy

As already mentioned, sex is only a part of intimacy. There is no doubt that sexual relations can create a strong bond between partners, especially initially, and the need for each other to provide gratification helps create that initial bond. However sex is not the only way to create a meaningful relationship that is beneficial to both partners. At times in our lives, sex is a very necessary part of our togetherness and at other times, it is not. The energy within our lives fluctuates. Our needs and desires fluctuate. All we need to do is be open to change, to the flow of life and to appreciate the gifts that each change brings. This is awareness practice in action.

153 D Cozort, *Highest Yoga Tantra*, Snow Lion Publications, New York, 1986.

A very necessary quality for intimacy is to be able to listen to the other person; to hear their story from their lips and heart and to be able to set aside oneself for the other. Sex may not always fit into this concept. Sex may imply that I want something for myself. A sexual relationship which neglects to identify the needs of both partners with regard to sex will not last. One can't have a sexual relationship alone – at least not the sort I'm referring to here - a committed long-term relationship with another close person. A sexual relationship can teach us to respect the rights and wishes of others whilst attempting to honour our own needs. Gradually over time, we learn that we can delay our desires if we need to; that we don't have to have what we want right this minute and that we can learn to be considerate of others. A sexual relationship can teach us much about pleasure, joy, relaxation, self-control, giving pleasure to another and respecting people's boundaries. We also learn to respect the commitments other people have made and not to intrude on that. An intimate relationship will not be possible if we desire to control the other or if we allow the other to control us. Control breaks trust, which stops intimacy: simple as that.

Learning Awareness Through Conflict and Differences

A close relationship over time can bring out the worst in us. We are shown, through the usual conflicts and differences, especially as the relationship progresses, where we are stuck with our personal growth. It is relatively easy to feel compassion, love and peace whilst sitting on a meditation cushion but it is quite another matter entirely to feel that same love and compassion in the midst of an argument about our day-to-day mutual decisions. The other person interprets reality differently. What one person may regard as a reasonable solution the other may find incomprehensible. Unless we have developed to the degree where we can look past the values, opinions and tastes of our partner to the loving person inside, we are bound to feel friction and annoyance from time to time.

Different Styles of Arguing

It is best not to have unrealistic expectations of a relationship. Our patterns of arguing (and therefore of communicating) date back to patterns learnt in our family of origin. If one learnt to suppress emotions, i.e. 'It's not safe to disagree or I won't be loved and I might be punished', then such a person will need to learn to be aware of this behaviour. Some people may have learnt to deal with conflict by using anger, others by avoidance, others by denial. We know when a conditioned pattern of responding is active because we don't have any control over the reactive emotion; in fact we go into a type of unconscious functioning. This tells us that we are acting out a learned behaviour pattern with its accompanying rigid neuronal circuits which result in automatic responses under certain conditions. Understanding that with all the will in the world and all the psychological techniques we have learnt, we still may not be able to change these patterns, requires a great deal of self-acceptance. In such a situation, humour (at and with oneself) is a better strategy to use than self-blame. The skill of awareness however, can minimise damage by helping us to be aware of our speech and how it impacts on others. In the same way, knowing how to repair damage by apology and forgiveness can be our greatest human strength in relationships.

It is quite clear that people have different styles of relating during an argument. There may be avoidance, anger, frustration, hurt, emotion and blame – and all because we have learnt to see the world through different eyes. When we notice huge amounts of energy going into defending ourselves, we need to look at what underlying beliefs and opinions are fuelling our high emotion. We may very well find that it is our ego fighting for its rights (and our ego is basically conditioning). If we insist on always being right, even though the argument may simply be about different tastes, then the relationship will suffer. What ideally happens when differences occur and what will bring the most balanced and reasonable solution is for both people to wait until their energies are calm and less reactive and they have had time to look at their underlying beliefs and patterns, before discussing a solution to their problem. This reduces the blind conditioned reaction and allows us greater awareness and more spaciousness around the issue, free of our emotional entanglements. We will also have had the time to reflect on what is most important – the love we have with our partner, or the need to be right thereby preserving our ego. Without a heart connection and a willingness to give when required, a satisfactory resolution will be difficult to achieve.

Communication Skills

Conflict can be a huge and powerful testing ground for the relationship. I would recommend to everyone, whether they are in a relationship or not, to develop some awareness of their communication skills. A wonderful book to begin with is Robert Bolton's *People Skills*.[154] He writes that we benefit from learning and becoming aware of our basic communication skills such as reflective listening, assertion skills, use of roadblocks (ordering, threatening, judging, name calling) and the dumping of our insecurities onto the other person. Also, if we can become more aware of what sets off conflict and begin to read the signs of impending conflict, we are more able to prevent it from escalating and more able to deal with it before it gets out of control. Our levels of tolerance and acceptance of others are important factors in how soon we lose control and begin an argument. Once again these are skills - we aren't necessarily born with them. We will help our ability to deal better with conflict by studying and practicing the skills of awareness training, by reflecting on our ego's beliefs, by practicing tolerance, and by speaking respectfully to others, even when we don't agree with them.

154 R Bolton, *People Skills*, Simon and Schuster, Australia, 1999.

Recognising Our Needs Beneath the Conflict

In Ike and Judith Lasater's book, *What We Say Matters*, we read that good communication is fundamentally about intention first.[155] The method of communication used is secondary, or follows on, from that. They make a salient point that in any difference of opinion, we first must understand what needs are being threatened in the interaction and understand where these needs are coming from, before we can listen to the other. The idea is that both people bring their particular needs to an interaction and the solution is often simply about understanding the needs rather than being right. For instance, our child wishes to stay up later and we wish him to go to bed. It appears that the conflict is about what is a reasonable time to go to bed but if we go deeper into what each person needs, it may be that the parent is tired and wants some quiet time while the child wants some control over the decisions made for him. Once these deeper needs are acknowledged it is easier to come to a resolution that goes some way towards meeting both needs. Before a resolution is possible though, we need to be in touch with ourselves so that we can truly understand what it is that we really need in this situation before expressing that in a non-violent manner. This is the principle of awareness on a slightly deeper level.

Harm Minimisation

In reality, being able to see through the other's differences takes a great deal of self-development and spiritual work, more than many of us achieve in a lifetime. It is quite rare to see people in a close relationship handle conflict perfectly. I have never met such an imaginary couple. Although we discuss conflict resolution or hear it discussed reasonably often in Western culture, the reality is that conflict resolution in intimate relationships can remain a difficult goal. We can however, learn to be aware of our patterns. It is possible to acknowledge that people have weaknesses,

155 J & I Lasater, *What We Say Matters*, Rodmell Press, California, 2009.

rather than judge them, and accept the existence of weaknesses, which can't yet be changed. It is through this acceptance and non-judgemental stance that people are encouraged to be aware of their weaknesses whilst keeping harm done to themselves and others to a minimum. This is living with eyes wide open – not avoiding or blaming and yet taking responsibility to do whatever one can in the circumstances to improve the situation.

Awareness of Speech

One very wonderful aspect of our contact with others is that we gradually learn from their reactions to what we say, how to be more compassionate. Awareness of speech is one area of self-growth that can be a struggle for many of us. Through a loving relationship, we can begin to see life through the other's eyes and through this we can come to understand how our choice of words affects them. Our speech may be culturally different from others depending on the nationality of our family of origin and also in how much we reveal or hide. Once again, awareness of how our speech affects others is very much tied in with how we grow in awareness generally. Relationships with others, especially honest friends and partners, can provide much fertile ground for improvement. In all cases though, a wish to resolve conflict must be powered by a desire for a meaningful interaction with the other person and vice versa. Without this basic goodwill interactions between people can become a battleground.

The Good Heart Versus Boundaries

Meditation can help with this intention to communicate respectfully. It works subtly on creating the good heart. The potential to learn and practice tolerance, forgiveness, simple allowing and non-judging of others are opportunities which present themselves again and again in relationship. This is not to allow or condone abuse of any sort in a relationship but to allow each person to be him/herself within acceptable boundaries in the relationship. The issue of where the boundaries are to be is an ongoing and never-ending process - a true masterpiece of negotiation between the two parties. Bear in mind that when we love another, we respect each other and don't allow ourself to be exploited or abused because it is harmful for both of us. This is the concept of non-violent resistance. Sometimes it is necessary to say no. This needs to be done clearly and without malice. Abuse is equally harmful for the perpetrator and the victim.

The Transient Nature of Relationships

All relationships change with time and all relationships end, either during life or with death. It is ironic that in our most loving relationships there is also the potential for the most pain at their ending. Our attachment to another creates an energetic melding which can result in huge personal loss and grief when such a relationship finishes. For some people the risk of this deep pain being overwhelming prevents them from actively seeking a new relationship. For some, the heart once broken never heals. Most of us however, keep plodding on. We continually expose ourselves to more relationship learning even though it may bring more pain. There is some seed inside which pushes us towards human connection, wholeness and self-development. We want life to be good and enjoyable and we know that human connection brings some degree of happiness.

There is no doubt in my mind that some close intimate relationships, after a reasonable period of trying to improve them, are better left. In some cases the two people involved receive no benefit and in some cases, receive harm from the other partner. People change over time. It may happen that one or both are no longer willing to try to repair the damage that may have occurred. This is a difficult call, always. We invest so much of our lives in intimate relationships. They become a huge part of our life history, our self-image and our view of reality. However, when there are too many negatives that can't be forgiven or changed and we lose our trust in the other person, we no longer feel safe. We become defensive and self-preservational. This is no environment for growth, love and happiness.

Often people in difficult relationships have built up patterns of relating together over many years. In the end, staying together or separating is usually a heart/mind decision, not based on logic alone. People sense that the energy of a relationship is not good and this can be easily seen in how the two people treat each other. We might also recognise in such a relationship that our inner energy becomes unbalanced. Some inner knowing will build up and become apparent until we cannot deny the truth any longer and we must act with courage to change our situation.

The Place of Acceptance

Relationship gives us a wonderful opportunity to practice in daily life what we are learning in spiritual practice. Every moment in relationship is a constant call to awakening. We have a choice between judging ourselves and another or loving ourselves and another. The two are mutually exclusive. One of the most valuable lessons is to learn to 'deeply allow' the other person to be, whilst at the same time supporting them to grow according to their own agenda. This means accepting the other person as he/she is and allowing that person their differences; in other words – loving their uniqueness. The more different the partner (friend/colleague), the more we can learn to love, without that partner having to think or act or even to like things that we do. Such a relationship tests our ability to commune with someone from the opposite point of view.

Acceptance is a powerful lesson and a partner can be a wonderful meditation. If we can touch, meet, embrace and share despite our differences, we have learnt much. The sense of connection that we gain from relationships gives us a powerful impetus along the path of learning awareness.

Johanna Engwerda

CHAPTER EIGHT
THE ESSENCE

1. Mindfulness/Awareness Practice

Awareness doesn't come about instantly like turning on a light globe. I sometimes liken it to the everyday processes of noticing many things. For many years I have walked in the area where I live, but it was not until one day recently that a tiny red and black bird landed on the path directly in front of me, wagging its tail. I stopped and really looked at this exquisite little creature and was filled with wonder. I went home and drew the bird with coloured pencils and then I looked it up on the internet. It had a name and so I became familiar with its appearance, habits and where it is to be found. Now I actively look for unusual birds when I go out to walk and I go to particular areas, especially in the early morning, where I know they are to be found. I really enjoy seeing birds. Why did I start noticing birds when I had already spent so many years walking without noticing them?

The first time we notice a beautiful bird or a perfect wildflower (or anything else) that we haven't noticed before, despite it being there, can be thought of as a chance happening. We happened to be in the right place at the right time. Or it may be that we are blessed with a sudden insight and appreciation of something beautiful. It is a moment of grace. This first noticing then sets off a spark of curiosity or interest and from there we cultivate a search to see and learn more about the bird or flower. We are blessed with a new interest – something that gives more meaning, gratitude and energy to our lives.

It is by being aware of all the little things that we gain more awareness of the big picture.

Meditation is a skill that can help us to notice more along the path of life. Most meditations begin with focusing the mind's attention on an object, which is mindfulness. This concentration is then balanced with a softening of the mind to include a more spacious feeling of awareness. As we develop the qualities of mindfulness and awareness in our meditation practice, we also gradually find it arising in our daily lives. It feels like an awakening to ourselves and what we see around us. The term 'enlightenment' in Buddhism actually means complete awakening.

Right now, as you read this, you have the ability to be mindful (focused on one thing - the words on this page) whilst being simultaneously aware (aware of the meaning of these words in the context of the whole book, aware of the sounds around you, aware of the time of day). It is this 'moment by moment' paying of attention that is so important if we are not to waste our lives. The essence of any spiritual or inner work is noticing and paying attention and then learning from what we notice – just as we do with noticing birds and wildflowers!

Mindfulness/awareness practice is the single most important work we will ever do in this lifetime. This is what Carl Jung means when he talks about bringing light into the darkness of our lives. Mindfulness/awareness practice, both spiritual and non spiritual, helps put life in perspective. It helps us to prioritise. It helps us to give a value to certain activities so that we use our life as though it is a precious gift and not waste our energy on negative events and behaviours. It builds gratitude for what we have. In the Tibetan Buddhist tradition awareness is also roughly translated as intelligence, a state of learning and understanding.

So where do we begin?

How do we go about sifting and sorting our lives? How do we refine our lives so that our precious energy is not scattered and lost? How do we know what to let go of? How do we build the useful, the healthy, the loving?

Once again the mind is running on. Firstly: notice that it is doing so, this is the first important step.

Then stop. Right now. Stop and breathe. Close your eyes if it helps get rid of distractions.

Do absolutely nothing except breathe.

After a while you will notice that while your body may be still, your mind certainly isn't.
This is fairly usual.

It is this running activity of the mind that prevents us from paying attention to each thing that we experience. We often just skim our attention over events and then we are onto the next thing. Have a couple of cups of coffee and see this effect of the scattered, running mind exaggerated. Our mind energy can easily become too wild (probably not helped by our busy external environment) and it needs to be trained.

Try sounding a gong or other long musical note and notice whether you are able to pay full attention to the sound until it completely disappears. Do other thoughts intrude before it is finished?

Close your eyes and pay attention to the movement of your abdomen as you breathe. How long is it before you start to think of something else?

Take a mouthful of your dinner. Can you taste, chew and enjoy that mouthful without thinking about anything else?

Listen to your child explain his latest difficulty with a friend. Can you pay attention to the conversation in its entirety or have your thoughts long gone to the job that you need to do next?

Do you walk to the car noticing the fresh air, the lovely clouds and the sound of the birds? Or is your mind occupied by your tasks on your list and your destination?

Do you worry about things whilst on your daily walk or are you able to enjoy being outdoors and the movement of your body?

Do you notice when you are ill, the frustration caused by the loss of power and control? Do you see how valuable an experience illness is in forcing you to stop and pay attention to the way you move your body or the things that cause you pain? Does the injury or illness help you to become more aware of your body? Or do you blame others and become bad-tempered?

All these are ways in which we can test our everyday ability to pay attention and to be aware. Mindfulness/awareness practice can make us feel more balanced or more centred; less fragmented and rushed, and less restless. We also begin to appreciate others, to respect others and to live with more care for all living beings. We eventually are happier or at least more content. We learn that we always have choices. We learn moderation or balance in all things. Mindfulness practice can appear too simple. In Western culture we value the complicated. Learning to recognise this desire for the sophisticated is part of mindfulness training.

Despite having a good Western education we can still be ignorant in many other ways. It is possible to peel away the layers of ignorance through meditation and other disciplines. We can come to the understanding that we are not separate from others and that we can become whole in our own presence. Mindfulness leads to the experience of the divine in everything. Another word for the divine is spirit and spirit is this quality of heightened consciousness. When we rediscover mindfulness we are able to experience that the divine is evident in a perfect little bird and a leaf or flower covered in early morning dew. The divine is evident in our partner, our child, the clouds, the home cooked dinner, the vivid colour of a fabric, the aroma of a spice. The divine is a mind state and once we learn to contact it, we can find it everywhere. Spiritual practices outline the path. All we have to do is practice with motivation and persistence.

2. Every Moment of Every Day is an Opportunity to Practice

At the end of each day, we can spend a few minutes reflecting on the day that has been and we can decide whether or not any activities or interactions have been meaningful to us, to our life satisfaction. Once we have done that, it is possible to conceive of new ways of spending the next day or changing our next day, even in a small way, so that how we spend it is more meaningful than the previous one. This change may be as small as changing our attitude to something that needs to be done. When we get up in the morning we can again spend some minutes, or longer, in quiet reflection, prayer, meditation, walking or other such activity and benefit from any inspiration that arises during this time. Often we notice little flashes of insight arising, which may help determine how to improve this current day. If we progress in this way, step by step, making small improvements in our mind and environment, then over time we can create more meaning in our lives – the key is to do it day by day and consistently.

If we look at a daily practice such as meditation, the qualities learned in formal meditation are gradually transferred into our everyday lives as small changes in our attitude, by a process which feels similar to osmosis. If we regularly immerse ourselves in the positive states of meditation, our mind becomes familiar with them and they are easier to access and sometimes arise spontaneously during the day when we are not meditating.

There is an ongoing energetic rebalancing occurring. Eventually life itself becomes the meditation. We can include everything: work, relationships and negativity as our practice. Awareness practice includes all of life. Everything becomes practice. There is no point having wonderful spiritual experiences but not being able to tolerate another's differences or be in a relationship. We begin to realise that our spiritual world is not separate from our material world. Inner work and outer work must eventually merge together. The conscious mind, the unconscious mind and natural mind must eventually be experienced as one with awareness. Importantly also, awareness is not just a mind-based exercise. It must be joined with the heart wisdom which is simple kindness. Awareness and kindness together have huge power to bring meaning into our lives by transforming us and our perception of the world we live in.

Progress on the path of self-development and spiritual awareness can be slow and it is important not to be discouraged. No matter how bad the day seems, as long as we maintain awareness, the day is not lost, we are still achieving something by practicing awareness. Yes – even in the midst of a 'give up' type of day! Every day offers opportunities for awareness/mindfulness practice. No day need ever be considered a wasted day.

I would like to recount my *Diary of a Bad Morning* which I look on now as a humorous story to read and which contains a very important lesson about using both the 'good' and the 'bad' in our awareness practice. The shadow side of ourselves is also fodder for practice. Becoming aware of our failings and allowing ourselves to really feel, accept and know them, is a wonderful practice. On this particular morning, I decided to write down what I was experiencing. Revisiting this experience taught me that no day is ever wasted as long as we keep noticing. The way we do this is by observing ourselves with honesty, as though we are watching someone else. Then the day becomes an opportunity to observe our thoughts and emotions. None of us are above having sick days, low times or bad times. It is part of being human. Read on and enjoy.

Diary of a Bad Morning

(Mindfulness in our everyday life)

1 am:

Still can't sleep. Am getting desperate. I'll get up for a while. I take one cold and flu tablet against my will. It has codeine in it which will knock me out (I hope). I don't want to take it but I haven't slept properly for weeks now. Perhaps it's still the restless legs. Who knows? My restless legs seems ok right now – I took a homeopathic nasal spray at 10 pm and I have the support stocking on my right leg, so why can't I sleep???

2 am:

Last time I noticed the clock. Asleep. No restless legs.

8.30 am:

Woke for the toilet. My husband is at work doing overtime and I am in bed feeling miserable. I was looking forward to us having a day together. I am not happy. I can't see the point in getting up. I go back to bed.

8.30-11 am:

Why get up? I will probably have another sleepless night tonight since I'm getting up so late today. My husband is not here. Why go through the repetitive round of exercise, cleaning, keeping myself occupied, trying to make myself feel better? Am I getting anywhere? I can't seem to get myself out of bed and I don't care. Am having the morning off – I feel as though I've given up. I'm having victim thoughts. I don't care. It's too hard to be perfect. No one phones. No one cares. Now that there are no distractions, no people and no sleep – what is left?
Who am I?
Do I even exist?
How can I write this book? I am hopeless. I have a headache – probably need water and a coffee. I will hide away if the phone rings or anyone comes to the door.

11 am:

Get up for coffee – feel a bit better.
Gee – that fresh air feels great.
I sit in the kitchen with the sliding door wide open and I breathe in life. Fresh air. Outside looks good. The garden looks inviting. The earth doesn't judge. It supports, waits, holds. I think I'll go outside.

11.30 am:

I make French toast. Something different.
It might cheer me up.
Yuk – it's terribly soggy. I can't eat it. What a waste.
I give it to the neighbours cats outside.
While out there I see the lovely white cosmos flowers in the garden. I go get my camera and take a shot.
How beautiful.

11.45 am:

I get dressed. Brush my teeth, comb my hair.
I'm ready for the garden. It is calling me.
I take yesterday's notes and some paperwork up to my meditation room. I think to myself – Gee. I could have spent this morning sorting out all my papers up here!
An opportunity missed.
Silly girl.

12 noon:

OK. I feel ok again.
The day looks ok.
I'll get out and do some weeding.
My husband will be home soon.
Perhaps we can go out for a run on the motorbike, except I expect he'll be the tired one now.
What is life all about?
And it comes into my head...
Can I be mindful on a bad day? Yes.
Can I make choices on a bad day? Yes.
Can I 'give in' on a bad day? Yes.
Does it really matter if every day isn't perfectly full of self-development activities and thoughts? No.
It seems to me that life is a natural cycle of yin and yang, up and

down, shadow side and light side.
Is this a necessary cycle?
What is this all about, this not sleeping?
Why am I so distressed?
I know that it will eventually sort itself out and it's not as though I have to go to work at the moment.

And then it comes to me. It's about losing control over my day and my life. When I don't sleep properly I also can't control the following day as I'm too tired to concentrate on the things I want to do. I am lethargic, lacking in energy.
I can't seem to stop what's happening with my sleep. I just can't get back into a normal sleeping pattern.
I am frustrated.

12.15:

I have an idea.
I do the energy mudra outside. The one that works on the lower chakra that is supposed to give one life energy.
I do it outside so that I will absorb energy from the earth and the sun.
Soon I have an idea of what lesson I need to learn.
I need to learn to 'let go'. Learn to accept lack of control. Learn that we can still be mindful – we can still do this practice – when we are simply too tired to do other practices.
Mindfulness brings acceptance, wisdom, peace, patience and gentleness with oneself. It brings kindness.
Gentle mindfulness is the answer.
I am reminded also that this observation, relaxing and acceptance of negative emotion is the Tibetan Vajrayana method of dealing with negative emotions. Don't be afraid to look them directly in the eye, don't suppress them, just observe them, relax within them and eventually see them as amusing.

*   *   *

Another big lesson that we can learn from this story is that no matter how much spiritual and self-development work we have done, there will always be patterns that we can't seem to shift, especially patterns of thinking and deep emotion. Some of these 'pathways' may be well and truly fixed in our brains and we may just have to learn to accept some things about ourselves that, for the moment at least, we can't seem to change. If we can understand our frailties and watch how we struggle with them, we can really understand that no one is perfect. If we can understand that about ourselves, then we can understand that about others and perhaps this knowledge will help us to live with more harmony and tolerance in our close relationships and in society in general.

I have recently experienced a back injury and through this I have again become much more aware of how I move and feel in my body which automatically makes me much more aware of 'checking in' with myself regularly to see how I feel before I do the next thing. Any physical discomfort, injury or illness can also be a real call to awareness in the present moment and a very valuable practice in itself. In fact any event in our day, especially the challenging events, can be wonderful reminders to watch and to be aware. Each day is important. Let's break life down to manageable proportions and work with what is in front of us this very day.

3. Daily Spiritual Practice or Inner Work

It is a pity that most of us wait until our middle age years before we begin to look at the larger picture of life. When we are younger we don't have time or we can't sit still. There is perhaps too much to do, too much distraction and too much temptation. We seldom make the time for inner work unless we are blessed with a creative gift, or sometimes life will temporarily force us to go within due to illness, a failed relationship or misfortune. But it seldom lasts and most of us seldom make contemplative or inner work a regular part of our day. Why is this so? It is possibly because we are not aware of the value of inner work and so we lack the motivation to do it. In a very basic sense, we are simply 'not aware' of our lives passing and how we are living each day or of the importance of each day. We are not aware of living this very moment, we are already thinking about the next interval of time and what we'll be doing then. We miss whole tracts of time. We are not aware that we have a choice, moment to moment, about how to be.

The reason that we need to do some inner work, reflection or spiritual practice daily is that it reorientates us again and again towards looking for the meaningful in life. It provides a daily reminder to look for opportunities to put our aspirations to grow as a person, into practice. We can also receive guidance through contacting our inner wisdom at this time of the day which is, in effect, dedicated to our development. We so easily forget if we are not constantly reminded. Our many habits tend to steer the course of our whole day. By the very act of sitting down to meditate, or doing any other type of inner work or practice, we make this mindset a habit, reminding ourselves daily to turn our minds in that direction of self-awareness and growth.

If we choose meditation as part of our inner work, it is probably best to begin such a daily practice with a short practice rather than attempt to sit for half an hour and then be discouraged. It is also important to mention that one will not usually see immediate results. Spiritual or inner work is a lifelong process and progress is measured in years. We can't see the finishing line and there is no final goal. The practice day by day is the goal.

It is never too late and one is never too old or too young to begin learning a spiritual or self-awareness practice. We spend our whole lives learning and this never stops. Even our last day on earth will provide opportunities for learning. If learning meditation, I suggest starting with a small practice; something like the following simple three minute meditation. It contains the principles of all meditation practices and it can be done by people of any religion. I usually begin to teach people to relax the body first which teaches awareness of body, and then I teach awareness of the breath through breath practices which gradually teaches awareness of the mind; and then I teach a more spacious awareness which includes and expands on the first two. This simple meditation introduces all three of these concepts and provides a framework on which we can build. Each section can be lengthened to provide a longer meditation when we wish to extend it. One section alone can provide the whole focus for meditation also, so this is a good starting point while we explore how it actually feels to meditate. Learning to meditate involves daily repetition. As with all skills, as one practices, it becomes easier.

THREE-MINUTE MEDITATION

Sit yourself in a straight-backed chair so that the whole of both feet comfortably touch the floor. Loosen any tight clothing. Use cushions if necessary for comfort. Take the phone off the hook (put the mobile phone on silent and away from your body).

Let's begin.

First Minute: Body/Posture

Allow the eyes to close gently and feel where the feet touch the floor. Take a moment to feel these sensations.
Now notice your knees and thighs and just allow them to flop out. Let them go.
Place the hands palm down on the thighs or in the lap or wherever they are most comfortable for you.
Feel the pressure of the buttocks where they touch the seat of the chair.
Notice where the back makes contact with the back of the chair.

Keep it upright but not stiff.

Notice both shoulders. Draw them back slightly then let them drop and relax.

Let the arms hang from the shoulders. Feel the hands relaxed and loose on the thighs or in the lap.

Notice how the neck supports the weight of the head.

Keep the head balanced directly over the spine.

Second Minute: Breath

Now become aware of your normal breathing rhythm. Just observing the breath. Feel the breath. No need to change anything. Just notice.

Notice how the chest expands and contracts with the breathing.

Notice how the chest moves as you breathe. Take a moment to feel the sensations.

If you like, take a longer breath in, fill your lungs with air and then breathe out like a sigh. As you breathe out, say to yourself 'let go' and feel the letting go as you do that.

Then return to noticing how your normal breathing feels.

Third Minute: Spacious Awareness/Mind

Now noticing how the whole body feels sitting in the chair. Take a moment.

Notice how the body is still breathing all the time, all by itself.

Notice any sounds that are present in the background. Notice the quality of the sounds. Listen.

Notice how your hands feel right now. What sensations are present?

Notice any thoughts flowing through your mind. Notice them come and then go. Let them flow through.

Be aware of everything around you right now and let it all be. Letting go. Relax. Just be with the silence.

* * *

Another type of inner work which I emphasise in this book is Jungian dream analysis, which works on illuminating the shadow aspects of our personality. Being Western, I have found it a wonderful complement to Eastern spiritual work. Such work can be done alongside any spiritual path; in fact it provides another 'view' with which to view our inner selves and our self-created suffering. This too can be a daily practice in its own right and no doubt individuals can find other meaningful therapies and practices which appeal to their own unique set of circumstances. It is for each of us to discover what it is that we need to work on to help us digest our lives and find meaning in them. I firmly believe in making our inner work a priority and giving it the importance of a daily time slot. By doing this, we can give ourselves time to reflect on what we truly want to learn or change about ourselves in this lifetime and set about beginning some of this learning and changing. Daily reflection, practice and persistence is the answer.

* * *

Through writing this book I wish to share my learning so that others will be inspired to find their own truth. In fact there are many facets to every explanation; there are many truths. We need to keep our mind open and flexible because new explanations will continually appear. Our knowledge and our world are rapidly changing. The wonderful thing about spiritual practice is that sooner or later we realise that the answers we seek are within each and every one of us. We just have to learn how to contact that place within and then to trust what we hear. This is own true nature, pure consciousness, the ground of all being.

Unfortunately, this creative spaciousness remains hidden until we learn to contact it; to sit in its presence. Guidance and support from teachers is helpful initially and at all stages of the path however, we need to take the reins ourselves eventually. We must move on into our own truth with gratitude for what we have learnt through others. The process of purifying the ego never really finishes in this lifetime. The process of spiritual maturation takes time and very few have attained it. This is because pure consciousness does not stabilise easily in the human condition. It is not a human characteristic. We are human and as such can contact both the lower and the higher aspects of existence. This is the gift of being born human; there is so much opportunity for growth. As we age we stop striving for perfection, the impossible really, and we appreciate the path and the journey. The path is the journey.

The 14th Dalai Lama explains that spirituality is a human journey into our internal resources with the aim of discovering who we really are in the deepest possible way and how to live with wisdom and compassion. We are all linked, so whatever effort one person makes to become more conscious spreads to all those around him/her and probably towards many more people that we never get to meet. To my mind, the most worthwhile things learnt on this planet must include the spiritual (not necessarily religious), otherwise life is unbalanced and has no meaning. It is the things of the spirit that keep us alive by affecting our subtle energy. Everyone can find something appropriate, some form of spirituality to digest and make use of.

The best way to digest life is to give it our full awareness. Developing awareness in many spheres of our being, as each chapter of this book has gone through, helps us to digest life in a wholesome and growth-encouraging way. What more could we want out of life than to say that we have learnt a lot and that we have been able to put that into practice for our benefit and for the benefit of others? That is a full, meaningful and valuable life!

APPENDIX A
Simple Meditation Using The Sensations Of The Body As A Focus

Preparation:

Sit in a chair with back upright, feet flat on the floor. Make sure you are warm and will be undisturbed. Gently close your eyes. Sit in the silence and notice how the body is mostly silent. Any noise comes from our speech and our thoughts as mental noise. Allow the mental noise to fade away and simply rest in the silence. Allow a minute or two.

Part A:

Now pay complete attention to the soles of the feet and how they feel at the moment. Keep the mind focused on these sensations. Do this for several minutes.

Now pay attention to the kneecaps of both legs and how they feel at the moment. Keep the mind focused on these sensations. Do this for several minutes.

Now keep both the sensations of the soles of the feet and the kneecaps in your awareness. Be aware of both at the same time. Do this for several minutes.

Now allow any noises from outside to enter into your awareness so that now we have the soles of the feet, the kneecaps and the sounds (perhaps of birds) in our awareness. We keep our attention 'circling' on these areas and say to any intruding thoughts 'not now'.

Part B:

Now pay complete attention to the area of the body at the base of the spine – the part of the back that is just above your bottom sitting on the chair. Focus on the skin and that outer part of the back, especially where it makes contact with the chair or cushion. Keep the mind focused on these sensations. Do this for several minutes.

Now pay attention to the upper chest; that area between the collarbones and the upper breasts. Notice any sensations there. Do this for several minutes.

Now keep both the sensations of the lower back and the upper chest in your awareness. Be aware of both at the same time. Do this for several minutes.

Now allow any noises from outside to enter into your awareness so that now we have the lower back, the upper chest and the sounds (perhaps of birds) in our awareness. We keep our attention 'circling' on these areas and say to any intruding thoughts 'not now'. Do this for several minutes.

Part C:

Now pay complete attention to the palms of the hands and how they feel at the moment. Keep the mind focused on these sensations. Do this for several minutes.

Now pay attention to the base of the skull; that area of the back of the head between the ears, especially where the skull bone ends and the neck begins. Notice how that area feels at the moment. Keep the mind focused on these sensations. Do this for several minutes.

Now keep both the sensations of the palms of the hands and the base of the skull in your awareness. Be aware of both at the same time. Do this for several minutes.

Now allow any sensations from the crown of the head to enter into your awareness so that now we have the palms of the hands, the base of the skull and the sensations in the crown of the head in our awareness. We keep our attention 'circling' on these areas and say to any intruding thoughts 'not now'. Do this for several minutes.

Rest:

Now we return to sitting in the silence. Most likely you will become aware of the body breathing. Perhaps you will be aware of the sounds outside. Just allow things to happen in the background of your awareness. As you sit in the silence notice also when any part of the body comes into your awareness. Simply allow sensations to come and go while you continue to rest in the silence. Do this for several minutes.

When your mind begins its thinking again, slowly open your eyes and gently gaze at the floor in front of you. Then, when you are ready, open your eyes, stretch and finish the meditation.

APPENDIX B
Body Relaxation Meditation

Sit yourself in a straight backed chair so that the whole of both feet comfortably touch the floor. Loosen any tight clothing. Use cushions if necessary for comfort. Take the phone off the hook or silence the mobile phone and move it away from your body.

And let's begin.

Allow the eyes to close gently and feel where the feet touch the floor. Take a moment to really feel these sensations.

Now notice your knees and thighs and just allow them to flop out. Let them go.

Place the hands palm down on the thighs or in the lap or wherever they are most comfortable for you.

Feel the pressure of the buttocks where they touch the seat of the chair.

Notice where the back makes contact with the back of the chair. Keep it upright but not stiff.

Notice both shoulders. Draw them back slightly and then let them drop and relax.

Let the arms hang from the shoulders. Fee the hands relaxed and loose on the thighs or in the lap.

Notice how the neck supports the weight of the head.
Keep the head balanced directly over the spine.

(1 minute)

Now work your way up the body from the feet to the head,
noticing how each area feels and then letting that area loosen
and soften. Do that a couple of times. Keep the back straight and
keep the chest open.

(2 minutes)

Now be aware of the chest moving as you breathe. Observe this
with your mind's eye allowing the breath to breathe at its own
pace and rhythm. Simply observe.

(1 minute)

Then take a deep breath in and as you breathe out, let go like a
sigh. Make the sound. Let the breath out slowly and fully. Do it
once more and as you breathe out, consciously let go in the legs
and the knees – softening and releasing.

Now be aware of the abdomen and how it moves with the
breathing. Just observe this happening.

(1 minute)

Then take a deep breath in and as you breathe out, let go like a sigh
letting go in the legs and the knees – softening and releasing.

Now be aware of the shoulders moving as you breathe. Just
observe this happening.

(1 minute)

Then take a deep breath in and as you breathe out, let go like a sigh letting go in the legs and the knees – softening and releasing.

Now be aware of all three areas of the body moving with the breathing simultaneously – the chest, the abdomen and the shoulders. Just observe this movement as you breathe.

(1 minute)

Now scan the body as we did in the beginning but this time work down the body from the head to the feet, noticing any tension and letting it go. Do that a couple of times, keeping the back straight.

(2 minutes)

Now let go of the technique or focus on the breath and simply sit in the silence. Relax. Feel the silence.

(1 minute)

And when you are ready, opening the eyes just a little and looking down at the floor in front of you. Notice how the body feels now. Notice how the mind feels now.
Gradually come out of the meditation.

APPENDIX C
Twenty Minute Breath Meditation

Place the body in a comfortable upright position with the feet flat on the floor and the back touching the back of the chair, buttocks tucked well into the chair, hands placed either on the thighs palm down or up or comfortably in the lap.

Place the attention on the soles of the feet for a few moments and notice the sensations there; allow the feet to soften.

Check the knees and thighs; let them flop out; let go of holding onto them. Feel the pressure of the buttocks against the seat of the chair. Notice the contact of your back with the back of the chair. Sense the shoulders; draw them back a fraction and then let them drop loosely. Allow the arms to hang heavily from the shoulders. Let the wrists be floppy, let the hands be loose and soft. Feel where the palms of the hands make contact with the clothes or skin.

Notice the sensations at the back of the neck and then at the back of the head. Travel the awareness across to the forehead; let it soften and smooth out. Let the jaw drop a little; let the face be soft and relaxed.

Travel down to the chest; notice the movement with the breath.

Check the abdomen; if there is any holding in, let it expand and relax. Let the whole weight of the body be supported by the chair and just let go; relax.

(3 minutes)

Then begin to notice the natural breathing rhythm. Just observe for a few moments, not changing anything, just sitting quietly.

(2 minutes)

Take a big breath in through the nose, filling the lungs completely and then a long slow breath out, through the mouth, a bit like a sigh (make a noise if you want, it works better) - and then return to normal breathing. Continue for a couple of breaths only.

(1 minute)

Take another big breath in (bigger than usual but not as big as before) and then as you breathe out (no sighing noise now), let go – sense a letting go of the breath and a letting go in the body as you exhale through the nose now. Feel the shoulders drop as you breathe out.

(continue for 2 minutes)

Take a good breath in and this time begin to lengthen the out breath. Keep the breathing easy and relaxed and comfortable.

(continue for 2 minutes)

Now change the focus to the out breath so that you are not really noticing the in breath anymore. Just notice each time you breathe out. Really observe how it feels to breathe out.

(continue for 2 minutes)

Now slow the out breath even more; slow it and let go completely.

Now when you follow the out breath; follow it to the very end of the breath. Notice when it's completely finished. Where does it end?

(continue for 2 minutes)

Notice that there is a pause or a gap at the end of the out breath.
Place all your attention on this pause, make it the focus now, and observe how it feels there and what happens there. What is your sense of this pause?
Does anything happen or does everything stop?

(continue for 2 minutes)

Now rest in that gap as long as is comfortable, until the next breath begins and flows in again of its own accord. Just relax with this process. Allow the breath to breathe itself. No need to control. Just let go. Just rest.

(continue for 2 minutes)

And now slowly open your eyes and look down at the floor in front of you.
Retain that sense of the breathing being relaxed and the body being relaxed.
Notice also how the mind feels now.

Sit quietly and then when you are ready, open the eyes fully and come out of the meditation by stretching the arms or legs.

(2 minutes, or as long as you like)

BIBLIOGRAPHY

J Baldwin, Notes of a Native Son, Beacon Press, USA, 1984.

R Bolton, People Skills, Simon and Schuster, Australia, 1999.

G Braden, The Divine Matrix, Hay House, USA, 2007.

G Braden, DNA Can Repair Itself With Feelings, Whispers From Beyond, issue 0042, published online, Eaton, Australia, December, 2008, retrieved 30 September 2011, <http://www.whispersfrombeyond.com.au/Newsletters/newsjan08article.htm>

Chogyal Namkhai Norbu, Dream Yoga and the Practice of Natural Light, Snow Lion Publications, New York, 2002.

Lam Kam Chuen, The Way of Energy, Gaia Books Ltd, New York, 1991.

D Cozort, Highest Yoga Tantra, Snow Lion Publications, New York, 1986.

Dalai Lama, The Universe in a Single Atom, Broadway Books, New York, 2005.

Dalai Lama, Sleeping, Dreaming and Dying, Wisdom Publications, Boston, 1997.

E D'Aquili & AB Newberg, The Mystical Mind, Probing the Biology of Mystical Experience, Fortress Press, Minneapolis, 1999.

N Doidge, The Brain that Changes Itself, Scribe Publications, Melbourne, 2008.

Pema Dorjee, Heal your Spirit, Heal Yourself, Watkins Publishing, London, 2005.

S Dowrick, Intimacy and Solitude, William Heinemann, Australia. 1992.

E Easwaran, Take Your Time, Nilgiri Press, California, 2008.

E Easwaran, Words to Live by, Blue Mountain Meditation Center, California, USA, 2005. <http://www.easwaran.org>

Friends of the Heart, The Sadhana of Vajrasattva for Foundation Practices, Friends of the Heart Meditation Centre, Toronto, 2001.

Friends of the Western Buddhist Order, Metta: the Practice of Loving Kindness, Windhorse Publications, Birmingham, 2000.

I Gawler, The Creative Power of Imagery, Hill of Content, Melbourne, 1997.

I Gawler, The Mind that Changes Everything, Brolga Publishing, Melbourne, 2011.

I Gawler, You Can Conquer Cancer, Michelle Anderson Publishing, Melbourne, 2001.

The Gawler Foundation, Cancer and Mind Body Research, retrieved 16 November 2011, <http:www.gawler.org/cancer-and-mind-body-research/>

D Goldberg & J Blomquist, A User's Guide to the Universe, John Wiley and Sons, New Jersey, 2010.

J Goldstein, Insight Meditation, Shambhala, Boston, 1994.

A Goswami, The Visionary Window, a Quantum Physicist's Guide to Enlightenment, Shambhala, Boston, 1994.

Lama Anagarika Govinda, The Way of the White Clouds, Rider, London. 1995.

R Guiley, Encyclopaedia of Mystical and Paranormal Experience, Grange Books, London, 1993.

E Harrison, Do You Want to Meditate? Perth Meditation Centre, Western Australia, 2002.

W Hartin, Why Did I Marry You? Hill of Content, Melbourne, 1988.

C Hassed, New Frontiers in Medicine, Michelle Anderson Publishing, Melbourne, 2005.

Independent Media Centre of Australia, Fighting for Positive Body Image for Young Women, retrieved 15 November 2011, <http://www.indymedia.org.au/2011/02/15/fighting-for-positive-body-image-for-young-women>

Heart Foundation of Australia, Food and Nutrition Facts, retrieved 16 October 2011, <http://www.heartfoundation.org.au/healthy-eating/food-and-nutrition-facts/Pages/fruits-and-vegetables.aspx>

HeartMath <http:// www.heartmath.org>

R Johnson, Owning Your Own Shadow, Harper Collins, New York, 1993.

R Johnson, The Psychology of Romantic Love, Arkana, Penguin, London, 1987.

C Jung, 'The Psychology of the Child Archetype', Collected Works, vol 9 part 1, Princeton University Press, 1969.

C Jung, Man and his Symbols, Penguin, Arkarna, 1990.

C Jung, 'Christ: a Symbol of the Self', Collected Works, vol 9 part 2, AION, Taylor and Francis, 1959.

C Jung, Memories, Dreams, Reflections, Collins, Routledge & P Kegan, London, 1963.

Kalu Rinpoche, A Rainfall of Blessing: a Guru Yoga, text from the enthronement celebration booklet to commemorate his reincarnation, Samdrup Sarjay Ling Tibetan Monastery, Sonada, Darjeeling, India, 1993.

Kalu Rinpoche, Gently Whispered, Station Hill Press, New York, 1994.

Kalu Rinpoche, The Dharma, State University of New York Press, 1986.

Kalu Rinpoche, Secret Buddhism, Clear Point Press, California, 2002.

Dilgo Khyentse, The Heart Treasure of the Enlightened Ones, Shambhala, Boston, 1992.

G Kieffer, Kundalini, Empowering Human Evolution: Selected Writings of Gopi Krishna, Triad Publications, Queensland, 1998.

Jamgon Kongtrul the Third. Cloudless Sky, Shambhala, Boston, 1992.

P Larsen & I Lubkin, 'Body Image', in 7th edit. Chronic Illness: Impact and Intervention, Jones and Bartlett, Massachusetts, 2009.

J & I Lasater, What We Say Matters, Rodmell Press, California, 2009.

J LeDoux, The Emotional Brain, Phoenix, London, 1999.

S Levine, A Gradual Awakening, Doubleday, New York, 1989.

BH Lipton, The Biology of Belief, Hay House, USA, 2005.

I McGilchrist, The Master and his Emissary: the Divided Brain and the Making of the Western World, Yale University Press, 2009.

K McLeod, Wake up to Your Life, Harper, San Francisco, 2002.

N Mehta, Indian Head Massage, Thorson, Harper Collins, London, 1999.

Mission Australia's National Survey of Young Australians, 2010, retrieved 15 October 2010, <http:// www.indymedia.org.au>

C Mitchell, Near Death, Mandarin, Australia, 1996.

GH Mullin, The Six Yogas of Naropa, Snow Lion Publications, New York, 2005.

D Murphy, A Return to Spirit, EJ Dwyer, Australia, 1997.

J Murtagh, General Practice, 3rd edit, McGraw-Hill, Australia, 2003.

Namgyal Rinpoche, The Breath of Awakening, Bodhi Publishing, Ontario, 1992.

New York Association for Analytical Psychology, About Jungian Analysis; Frequently Asked Questions, retrieved 8 September 2011, <http://www.nyaap.org/about-jungian-analysis>

M Nicoll, Dream Psychology, Samuel Weiser, Maine, 1987.

R Preece, The Psychology of Buddhist Tantra, Snow Lion Publications, New York, 2006.

C Rathbun, Clear Heart, Open Mind, Friends of the Heart, Toronto, 2008.

R Ray, Indestructible Truth, Shambhala, Boston, 2002.

R Ray, Secret of the Vajra World – the Tantric Buddhism of Tibet, Shambhala, Boston, 2002.

M Ricard, Happiness: a Guide to Developing Life's Most Important Skill, Atlantic Books, London. 2007.

M Ricard & Trinh Xuan Thuan. The Quantum and the Lotus, Three Rivers Press, New

York, 2001.
L Rosenberg, Breath by Breath – the Liberating Practice of Insight Meditation. Shambhala, Boston, 1999.
O Sacks, Awakenings, Picador, London, 1991.
J Sanford, Dreams and Healing, Paulist Press, New York, 1978.
J Sauer, The Perfect Day Plan, Allen and Unwin, Australia, 2009.
Z Segal, J Williams & J Teasdale, Mindfulness-based Cognitive Therapy for Depression, The Guilford Press, New York, 2002.
State Government of Victoria, Better Health Channel, Fact sheet: Meditation, retrieved 8 June 2011, <http://www.betterhealth.vic.gov.au/bhcv2/bhcarticles.nsf/pages/Meditation>
A Storr, The Essential Jung, Fontana Press, London, 1998.
M Talbot, The Holographic Universe, Grafton Books, London, 1991.
Tenzin Wangyal Rinpoche, The Tibetan Yogas of Dream and Sleep, Snow Lion Publications, New York, 1998.
Tenzin Wangyal Rinpoche, Tibetan Sound Healing, Sounds True, Boulder Colorado, 2011.
Tenzin Wangyal Rinpoche, Awakening the Sacred Body, Hay House Publishers, USA, 2011.
Tenzin Wangyal Rinpoche, Healing with Form, Energy and Light, Snow Lion Publications, New York, 2002.
Thubten Yeshe, The Bliss of Inner Fire, Wisdom Publications, Boston, 1998.
W Tiller, Conscious Acts of Creation, the Emergence of a new Physics, Pavior Publishing, California, 2001.
W Tiller, 'What are Subtle Energies?' Journal of Scientific Exploration, vol. 7, No. 3, 1993.
V Wallace, & A Wallace, A Guide to the Bodhisattva's Way of Life by Santideva, Snow Lion, New York, 1997.

Digesting Life Creating Awareness
Johanna Engwerda

		Qty
ISBN 9781922036469		
RRP	AU$29.99	.....
Postage within Australia	AU$5.00	.....
	TOTAL* $_____	
	* All prices include GST	

Name: ....

Address: ....

....

Phone: ....

Email: ....

Payment: ❏ Money Order ❏ Cheque ❏ Amex ❏ MasterCard ❏ Visa

Cardholders Name: ....

Credit Card Number: ....

Signature: ....

Expiry Date: ....

Allow 21 days for delivery.

Payment to: Better Bookshop (ABN 14 067 257 390)
                   PO Box 12544
                   A'Beckett Street, Melbourne, 8006
                   Victoria, Australia
                   admin@brolgapublishing.com.au